Table of C

ABOUT THE AUTHOR

Mary English was born in London and educated in Switzerland at the American International School of Zurich. She comes from a large family and is one of five children. She is an Author, Astrologer, Homeopath and Hypnotherapist.

She lives and works in Bath U.K.

Her books include: *6 Easy Steps in Astrology, The Astrology of Indigos; Everyday Solutions to Spiritual Difficulties, The Astrology of Lovers; How Astrology Can Help You Love Better, A Little at a Time, Homeopathy For You and Those You Love*

Mary is also the author of 12 Sun sign books: *How to Survive a Pisces, How to Bond with an Aquarius, How to Cheer up a Capricorn, How to Believe in a Sagittarius, How to Win the Trust of a Scorpio, How to Love a Libra, How to Soothe a Virgo, How to Lavish a Leo, How to Care for a Cancer, How to Listen to a Gemini, How to Satisfy a Taurus and How to Appreciate an Aries*

She writes a monthly Sun sign column for the local publication Pukka Bath and for her Newsletter subscribers.

She also broadcasts her weekly Podcast: *Learn Astrology with Mary.*

She is a reformed Pisces.

PRAISE FOR NEPTUNE IN PISCES, AN ASTROLOGICAL SEARCH FOR ENLIGHTENMENT

"It is an honor to recommend Mary English's new book. Her clear and original writing also contains the personal warmth she shows in her podcasts. As a psychologist, I value her ability to perceive herself and others clearly in a deeply accepting manner."

Ruth Kanost, PhD.

Neptune in Pisces

An Astrological Search for Enlightenment

Mary English

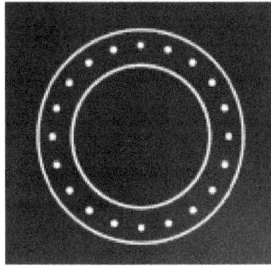

Future Path Publishing
Bath, U.K.

Future Path Publishing
Bath, U.K.

Cover Design: Izzi Daly

Dedication

This book is dedicated to my mother
Jean Madalon English nee Latham 1921- 2013
Who was always excited to hear I had written a book.

*You may still be debating which planets are your keynotes. Chances are, if you're this deeply into astrology, that one of them is either Uranus or Neptune. Astrology is ruled by Uranus, but many astrologers are Neptunian. How can you tell which of the two types people are? Ask them what day it is today. If they look at their calendar watches, they're Uranian. If they look **for** their calendar watches, they're Neptunian.*

Donna Cunningham, *How to Read Your Astrological Chart, Aspects of the Cosmic Puzzle*

Preface

As a professional Astrologer I am extremely interested in the night sky but unlike Astronomers, who explore the vastness of deep outer space, stars and galaxies Astrologers concentrate on only our immediate solar system. This includes the Sun, the Moon, which orbits us, then we both orbit the Sun.

And the other celestial bodies: Mercury, Venus, Mars, Jupiter and Saturn, which do too.

In our solar system there are three other outer planets that were only discovered when telescopes were invented: Uranus, Neptune and Pluto.

Neptune was the second to be found.

This book is about Neptune and my experience of it astrologically passing over my Sun and Mercury, while it was in the sign of Pisces: my Sun sign.

The Fuzzy Road to Neptune's Identification as a Planet not a Star.

Neptune was nearly discovered by Galilei Galileo (Sun Pisces, Moon Taurus) who first saw it while he was observing the Jupiter system on 28th December 1612.

His natal chart is very interesting as he had Sun conjunct Pluto, the same signature as the person who eventually identified Neptune.

In 1781 German-born amateur astronomer and musician William Hershel (Sun Scorpio, Moon Capricorn conjunct Uranus), discovered Uranus while living in Bath, U.K. where I live. His sister, Caroline (Sun Pisces, Moon Cancer) helped him. After this discovery, astronomers continued to observe the night sky and track the movements of other celestial bodies.

Neptune's discovery *wasn't* made just by telescopic observation. The astronomers who were working on the case used 'mathematical astronomy'. Uranus wasn't moving as predictions said it should, so they concluded that *another* planet must be affecting its orbit.

Neptune was recorded several more times, without being recognized as a planet, for a few more years.

Then Joseph Hyérosme Lefrançois de Lalande a French astronomer (Sun Cancer, Moon in Aquarius), recorded Neptune on the 8th and 10th of May 1795 again thinking that it was a star.

William Herschel's son (Sun Pisces, Moon Taurus) John Herschel, who was involved with the discovery, recorded Neptune on 14th July 1830 also believing it to be a star.

Eventually another Pisces (Sun conjunct Pluto the same as Galileo): Urbain Jean Joseph Le Verrier who worked at the Paris Observatory, used mathematical calculation to prove its existence and:

"discovered a star with the tip of his pen, without any instruments other than the strength of his calculations alone."

Urbain received many honors and widespread recognition for his achievement.

The Times carried the headline on the 1 October 1846: *"Le Verrier's planet found".*

Name: ♂ Urbain Le Verrier [Adb]
born on Mo., 11 March 1811
in St.Lô, FR
1w05, 49n07

Time: 10:00 a.m.
Univ.Time: 10:04:20
Sid. Time: 21:12:41

ASTRO·DIENST
www.astro.com
Type: 2.GW 0.0-1 5-Jun-2021

Natal Chart (Method: Web Style / equal)
Sun sign: Pisces
Ascendant: Gemini
Transits 31 Aug. 1846

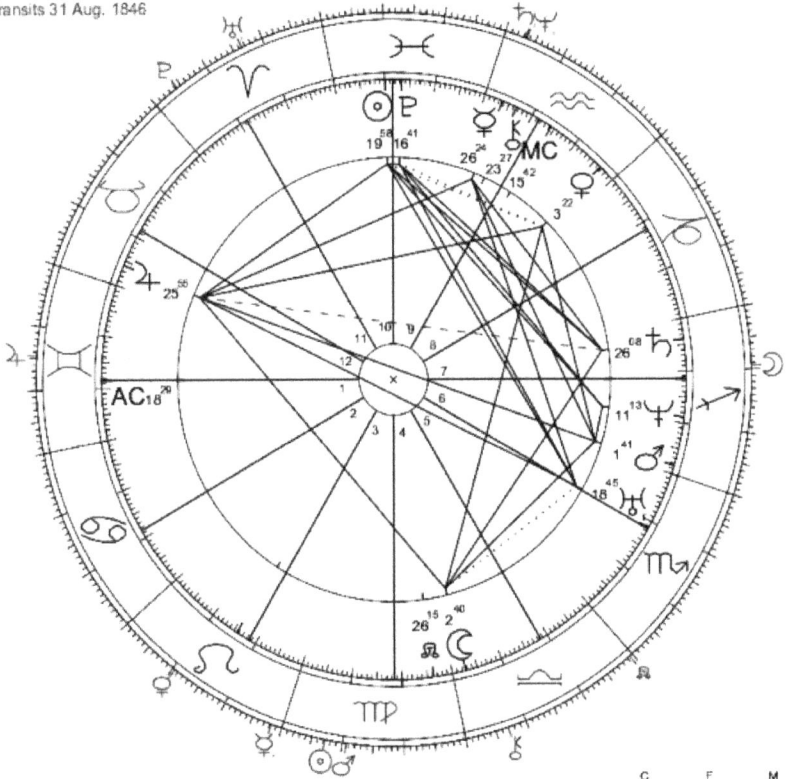

	Natal	Transit
⊙ Sun	19 Pis 56' 2"	7 ♍ 10'
☽ Moon	2 Lib 39'47"	20 ♐ 35'
☿ Mercury	26 Aqu 23'33"	28 ♌ 14'r
♀ Venus	3 Aqu 21'57"	10 ♌ 24'
♂ Mars	1 Sag 40'33"	10 ♍ 36'
♃ Jupiter	25 Tau 55'10"	14 ♓ 40'
♄ Saturn	26 Sag 7'30"	26 ♒ 42'r
♅ Uranus	18 Sco 44'32"r	13 ♈ 34'r
♆ Neptune	11 Sag 12'43"	26 ♒ 28'r
♇ Pluto	16 Pis 40'40"	25 ♈ 44'r
☊ True Node	26 Vir 14'39"d	29 ♎ 28'
⚷ Chiron	23 Aqu 27' 6"	7 ♎ 2'
AC: 18 Gem 28'37"	2: 18 Can 29'	3: 18 Leo 29'
MC: 15 Aqu 42'13"	11: 18 Ari 29'	12: 18 Tau 29'

Chart showing natal planets with the transits for the date Le Verrier announced his discovery.

3

You could say it was people born into the sign Pisces that were mostly involved in the discovery and identification of their Ruling planet. Which up until that point had been associated with Jupiter.

All the signs of the Zodiac have a planet that looks after them. We call them their Rulers. It's an ancient Astrological custom and comes from imagining the attributes of each planet and aligning them with each sign of the Zodiac. It certainly isn't a scientific fact. A lot of Astrology is creative.

Another astronomer (Gemini) John Couch Adams also worked independently on 'finding' the planet.

As discovering a new planet in our solar system was such an important find, there was plenty of disagreement between the two countries Great Britain and France over who had priority for the discovery. Eventually, after considerable argument, it was decided to give the credit to both Urbain Le Verrier *and* Adams.

The planet didn't get called Neptune until 29th December 1846.

Astrology is the study of planetary movements in relation to human affairs. As above, so below.

Astrologers therefore have had at least 174 years to work out the *meaning* of this planet.

A Brief History of Astrologer's Thoughts on Neptune

In 1903 Alan Leo an avid professional Astrologer, so into his subject he changed his name from William Frederick Allan to his Sun sign of Leo, published a book called *Astrology for All* 1.

As Neptune had only been discovered 57 years previously, Astrologers had a slightly less positive attitude to this planet.

Here he is talking about Neptune:

"Neptune is esoterically said to represent those who are endeavouring to realise that which is called the Platonic life. In the world to-day,

strangely enough, its evil side shows in frauds, cheats, charlantaury, illusions and deceptions. Gigantic swindles come under Neptune."

By 1938 in his *The Art of Synthesis* 2 he admits he still doesn't know as much about Neptune as he does about Uranus:

"It may be safely stated that astrologers are quite familiar with all temperaments coming under the various planets, save those which belong to the Uranian and Neptunian group. Of these two much more is known of the former than the latter, but so far as experience goes up to the present, Uranus and Neptune appear to represent the two extremes of a certain temperament which may be termed, for want of a better word the spiritual."

By 1951 Margaret E. Hone author of *The Modern Text Book of Astrology* 3with a nod to Alan Leo writes about Neptune:

"Keywords: Nebulousness, Impressionability.

This planet has to do with what hides itself from view, hence it is the most difficult for which to find a suitable one-word description.... Ether was first used for surgery in 1846. Gas began to be used for lighting...like all Neptunian things, they are elusive. The non-materiality leads to connection with intangibility, hence ideas of spirituality come under this rulership. The depths of confusion may be reached, or the heights of mysticism...A key to the understanding of the ability to dissolve the bounds of the material worlds and to act under the inspiring urges from the intangible, which seem to come through the unconscious, giving contact with the world of inspiration in art, in dreams, in trance, in hypnosis and kindred states..."

By now Neptune is getting more of an identity, but it's taken more than 100 years to get to this place. Neptune's Astrological description continues to evolve.

In 1967 Colin Evans writes in The New Waite's Compendium of Natal Astrology 5.

NEPTUNE: mysticism, vagueness, fantasy, imagination, clairvoyance.

In 1970 historian Christopher McIntosh writes in his *Astrology, The Stars and Human Life, A Modern Guide* 4.:

"Astrologers regard it as an elusive and intangible force. 'Hidden' is the key word for Neptune. It has to do with everything that operates behind the scenes, vicariously, or in disguise. It tends also to represent spiritual and non-material energies. The modern astrologer, Charles E. O. Carter, says in his book, The Principles of Astrology, that Neptune 'commonly produces extreme sensitivities, physical and emotional, and is not only prominent in the nativities of musicians, but also of mediumistic persons."

Then in 2006 Pisces Richard Tarnas in his wonderful book *Cosmos and Psyche, Intimations of a New World View* 6 firmly identifies Neptune's character:

"The archetypal principle linked to Neptune governs all nonordinary states of consciousness as well as the stream of consciousness and the oceanic depths of the unconscious. Characteristic metaphors for its domain include the infinite sea of imagination, the ocean of divine consciousness, and the archetypal wellspring of life."

Connecting with Divine Consciousness

It is this association with 'the ocean of divine consciousness' that I will be exploring in this book.

When I was in my early twenties I had a mystical experience brought on accidently by starvation, lack of sleep and extreme worry: I literally 'saw the light'.

I recorded my exploration to rediscover that light without having to starve or affect my mind or body in such a radical way.

Astrologers associate Neptune with the sign of Pisces. I wrote this book while 'under the influence' of Neptune being in or as we call it: transiting through the sign of Pisces. The present cycle started in February 2012 and ceases at the end of March 2025.

The last time this happened was from April 1847 to February 1862

I originally started this book as a daily record from July 2019 when Neptune was 18 degrees into the sign of Pisces. I was planning on only recording for 30 days to see if I could in any way 'connect with the divine'.

I even titled the book: *30 days with Neptune* but after 30 days I realised it was going to take far longer than that!

I finished the diary entries in June 2020 when Neptune was 20 degrees retrograde into Pisces.

In my own chart I have Sun 15 degrees in Pisces and Mercury retrograde 24 degrees in Pisces. The journal entries cover the major transit from my natal Sun to my natal Mercury.

I finally finished the book when Neptune was retrograde 23 degrees Pisces and Jupiter was retrograde 1 degree Pisces

Bath, July 2021

Introduction

I started my record in quite a positive state of mind. I'd decided originally to record Neptune's transits for 30 days. But as the record progressed I realised I didn't have the commitment to write it everyday. As the transit progressed I became more and more confused about which day was which and where I was in my record.

There were days when I didn't record anything. Then when I did, I would beat myself up for not writing anything earlier.

It felt a little like juggling.

Having to concentrate on Neptune's energies while also writing in sensible-enough English, what was happening for me.

I have divided the record into chapters, when in 'real life' there were no chapters and at that time, nothing I could make concrete and readable.

Throughout the whole process I analysed what I was recording in professional Astrological terms, making 'sense' of what was happening using Astrological interpretations.

However, as I got further into 'being' part of Neptune, I became less aware of what was actually happening in my own chart and could only record how I felt.

Chapter One

Good Intentions

Day One
Sunday 28th July 2019 17.55

Had a teeny nap earlier and dreamt about a woman I know. She had recently had a baby and was breastfeeding it. She was sitting opposite some nuns. One of the nuns helped her smooth down the back of her clothing, after I'd asked if she needed any help. Then as she was feeding the baby, one of the nuns turned away from her, as if she didn't want to see anything...

I was in a building and my worry was too many people were walking around it. I told someone I was with that I didn't like knowing so many people were there, in my space, being allowed to be there. I laid some of my clothing on a seat to make it known that the seat was mine, in the hope that no-one would sit on it.

As if because it was my home and my space, uninvited visitors were not what I wanted.

As if my home had become a sort of guest-house and I was just a lodger there, not the owner.

How does one connect with the Divine? What tricks need to be activated? Do people really contact the Divine or have it come through them?

What is this 'voice' that can be heard, where truth is spoken? Do I need to do anything drastic for this to happen?

I know Neptune represents the Divine. It's not associated with any particular religion or faith.

It can manifest that way, which is why I want to also find that connection.

Surely this is something anyone can find, if they look hard enough?

I get up and close the door because the sound of my husband washing up in the kitchen is distracting my flow. And I want to be in the flow.

I've been battling with another book for months now and I just don't seem to be able to get it into any sort of order. At the moment it's a complete muddle. Bits here, bits there. Nothing concrete.

I know about Neptune and I also know that the present transit I am under will never happen again in my lifetime and I really, so, so much want to make the best of this, as it will never, ever happen again as long as I live.

That feels such a dramatic thing to say, but it's so true.

Neptune takes hundreds of years to traverse all the way through all the signs of the Zodiac. When I was born it was in the sign of Scorpio. Now it's in my sign: Pisces. And Neptune has an affinity with my sign. They're Astrological buddies.

They get along.

At this precise moment, Neptune is retrograde. So is Mercury and I thought it would be an opportune time to commence writing this as I was born during a Mercury retrograde, and maybe, just maybe Neptune will 'speak' through me or more accurately, through my writing while this happens.

I pause for a few seconds and look out of the window. A black car passes from my left to my right. Another one goes past. Same colour. Then a young man walks past going the other way. It's as if everything that happens while I'm writing is important.

How can it *not* be important if I'm allowing myself to be channelled through?

My problem is, I don't want to connect with God or Jesus or anything Christian.

I left that life-style having rejected it fiercely in my teens and early twenties. The result of a heavily religious upbringing is, either you accept the religion, or you reject it. There doesn't seem to be any middle-ground.

My spelling has gone to pot, and I've had to correct the words in the last sentence.

I'm finding noise distracting. I know perfectly well that in a few minutes any distractions will go as I become more involved in writing.

I truly think that writers definitely do need a certain sort of quiet while they write.

I'm aware that my Gemini Moon wants to move away from the page until he stops. I put on my headphones but they're light and hardly block my ears...

I want to connect with something Pagan.

Something older than religion.

Different to God, because after all, God has a really bad rap these days.

I call it the Divine, but even that sounds pretentious and I want to be real, and I want this experience to be real.

I've set myself the task to write everyday for one whole month and just keep myself open to how Neptune might communicate with me, through me or through the writing I am doing.

I'm not a very fast writer. I have to look at the keyboard. I'm certainly not a touch typist like my mother was.

She converted to Catholicism when she as 16. And so when she met my Dad when they were both 31, they had that in common. I quickly check the planets for that date and find that her conversion coincided with transiting Neptune conjuncting her natal Jupiter in the 4th.

Neptune at work again...

I wonder what voice Neptune has? Is it gruff, or sprightly or sing-song-y?

Does Neptune even have a sound?

If I open myself to communicate with a planet, in what way will that happen?

I've already mentioned my dream but I certainly can't write while I'm asleep and I don't feel happy going into a trance to do this. I know people have done that in the past.

I want to be awake, conscious, rational and aware.

Now I'm questioning whether or not that's possible as those aren't Neptune types of words.

Neptune is all about being woolly, or deceptive or deluded on the negative side.

While on the positive side it's about connection with something 'bigger' more expansive, more spiritual.

Not

Of

This

Earth.

How can I connect with that and retain my sanity and my ability to function in an everyday world in an everyday way?

Is that possible?

My questions seem petty.

As if I'm sort of challenging this entity to make an appearance.

As if I'm saying:' Well, if you were *really* there, you'd make yourself known'.

I don't want to do that either.

Be challenging.

Maybe I need to be inviting.

Maybe if I just put a message out to the Universe that I'd like to contact the spirit of Neptune, something will happen somehow that will bring that about.

All I have to do is ask and it will ...I was going to write 'be given' but I don't want to quote bits of the Bible as that's not my story.

My story is how Astrology is the answer (literally) to Life, the Universe and Everything. As fellow Pisces author Douglas Adams wrote about in his *Hitchhiker's Guide to the Galaxy.*

For me, it answers so many questions and gives me wonderful explanations for why people are the way they are and why events happen when they do and many other things.

With Astrology I feel as if I have a method to solve (almost) every human problem.

And Ha!

I'm having a big problem today connecting with one of the major planets.

Ha Ha!

I suppose though it isn't that easy to connect with a planet and if it was, everyone would be doing it. And anyway what makes me think I can do it any easier or quicker than anyone else? And what does speed have to do with it?

I've been writing now for just under an hour.

Maybe I need to sign-off for today and only hope that tomorrow brings more clarity or connection.

I can't believe I've set myself this task!

Not exactly a 'normal' thing to do but I'm not going to go there with worries about normality. Being normal is a subjective thing. Who says what is normal anyway?

Day Two

Monday 29th July 15.30

Can't remember my dreams. Got woken up early as we were going for a walk with Isobel our dog while the weather was cooler. Had a nice walk and tea in the sun afterwards.

Still sunny now. Put the fan on as it's a little hot in my office today. 24C

Not as hot as last week but warm enough to benefit from a breeze.

Been thinking about the Divine and maybe I need to define what I mean by Divine.

According to my trusty dictionary, divine is: from, or like God or a god, sacred.

And God is: superhuman being worshipped as having power over nature and human affairs. (**God**) creator and ruler of universe in Christian and other monotheistic religions, personal greatly admired or adored.

Monotheism: doctrine that there is only one god

Doctrine: what is taught, body of instruction; principle of religious or political etc belief

None of that really means much to me.

Who would want to take any instruction from someone or something that has 'power' over anything?

Can't say I really like that power bit.

Why can't the Divine be something that's sacred without it sounding so masculine?

I like the word sacred: connected with religion.

Religion: belief in superhuman controlling power, esp in a personal God or gods entitled to obedience and worship, particular system of faith and worship, thing that one is devoted to.

Devotion: great love or loyalty, enthusiastic zeal, religious worship.

Sometimes I really hate the English language.

I just don't see God as any of those things and I certainly am not going to devote my 'self' to something that commands obedience!

Crickey, that word rather hit a nerve with me...

Why can't contacting the Divine involve something a little more soft and less aggressive and order-making?

My last sentence disappeared when I went to correct a typo, this sentence is not the same as the previous one.

Is something trying to get through now?

How long do I have to focus on this subject before I get a connection?

Ha!

It's a bit like phoning someone's number and to keep getting the engaged tone!

Whoever or whatever is out there, or even in here, or maybe even in me is being rather hard-to-get.

I do know that the process of contacting the Divine does NOT involve badgering them/it or pleading.

I do know already that this segment of higher consciousness exists within all of us. I'm just trying to make contact in a rational, practical and creative way.

I'm asking for some insight.

I have been here before.

I was 21 when I last got into a weird spiritual experience.

But it involved a big amount of suffering and I don't want to suffer like I did then.

I would like to reconnect with the Bright White Light I saw then and to feel the connection without being scared out of my mind.

There's only one letter difference between sacred and scared.

I was so scared then.

But I don't want connection to be like that.

I want it to feel 'right' and 'welcoming' and maybe even 'wondrous'. Joy.

That would be a nice emotion to experience surely?

I've come across all sorts of religions in my life and I've had relatives who have converted to various faiths.

Their conversion is wondrous for them, but rather irritating for those at the receiving end of it, especially when their conversion involves them acting as if they 'know' something that we don't.

I'm not into that.

Connection to the Divine would be, should be something we can all experience.

No?

For those that want to?

Why do all these religions that have been created over the years involve some bloke getting in contact with 'god' up a mountain, or in the desert or under a tree? And everyone else following them because they had this weird experience?

Why can't connecting the Divine involve something we call all tap in to?

Surely whoever is there, or whatever it is, would want all of the human race to have an equal chance of doing this?

No?

Surely we don't have to be bonkers in the process or take loads of drugs or get off our faces with alcohol or prayer?

Why can't it involve just being aware and listening for connection?

Or watching?

Or feeling?

I'm getting a bit impatient again.

I want 'ta da' for something wondrous to happen....but why should it?

All I am doing is writing on the screen in my home office.

I'm not even writing with pen on paper...

Does God or the Divine even know about computers or even want us to discover it/him/her/them this way?

I sigh.

I know the shortest sentence in the Bible is 'Jesus wept.'

And he had a whole lot of weirder experiences than me, that's for sure.

I'm just an ordinary Astrologer wondering if a Neptune transit will allow me to ...

I stop for a few moments to check Rudolph Steiner's chart because he was also a fellow Pisces...

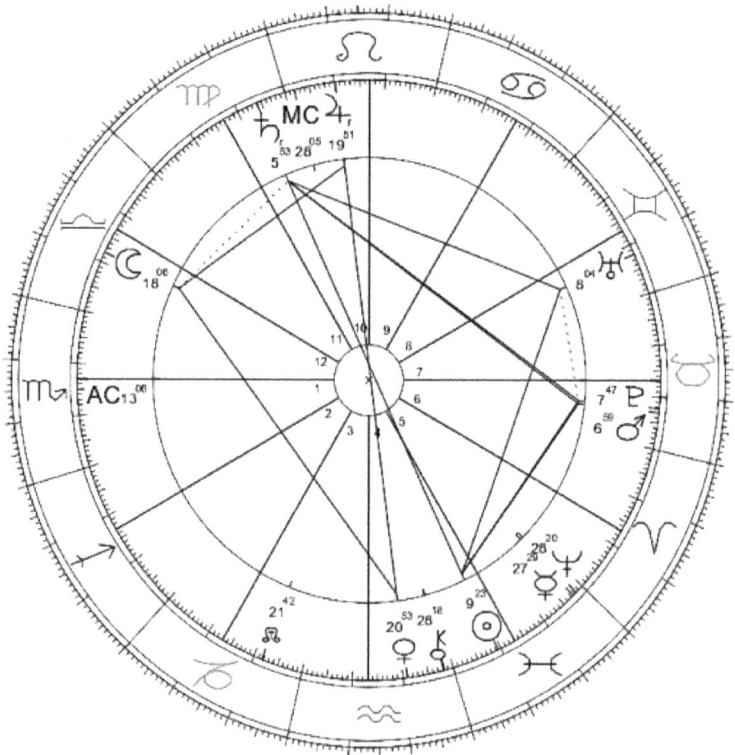

Name: ♂ Rudolf Steiner
born on We., 27 February 1861
in Darmstadt, GER
8e40, 49n53

Time: 11:30 p.m. LMT
Univ.Time: 22:55:20
Sid. Time: 10:01:00

ASTRO DIENST
www.astro.com

Type: 2.GW 0.0-1 5-Jun-2021

Natal Chart (Method: Web Style / equal)
Sun sign: Pisces
Ascendant: Scorpio

☉ Sun	9 Pis 22'57"		
☽ Moon	18 Lib 6' 1"		
☿ Mercury	27 Pis 26'40"		
♀ Venus	20 Aqu 52'43"		
♂ Mars	6 Tau 58'45"		
♃ Jupiter	19 Leo 51' 9"r		
♄ Saturn	5 Vir 52'35"r		
♅ Uranus	8 Gem 4'24"		
♆ Neptune	26 Pis 19'50"		
♇ Pluto	7 Tau 46'51"		
☊ True Node	21 Cap 41'31"		
⚷ Chiron	28 Aqu 17'32"		
AC: 13 Sco 6'15"	2: 13 Sag 6'	3: 13 Cap 6'	
MC: 26 Leo 4'34"	11: 13 Vir 6'	12: 13 Lib 6'	

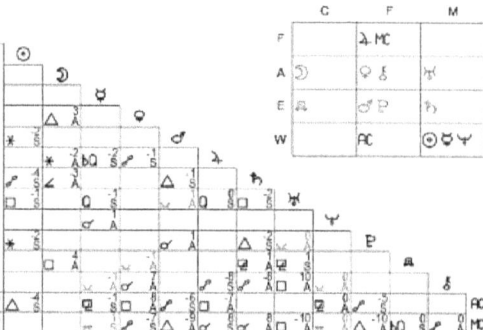

I thought so.

He was born in 1861 as a Sun 9 degrees Pisces, when Neptune was 28 degrees into the sign of Pisces.

His Mercury at 27 degrees Pisces was only one degree away from Neptune, and we call that a conjunction.

He wrote numbers of books about his spiritual experiences. I just recently read one of his books but because I read it on my Kindle I can't remember the title or too much of what it was about. I know I enjoyed reading it though.

That sounds awfully lame.

Enjoying a book but not knowing what it was about.

I do know that his writing can be hard to read as it's very wordy and lengthy...and as he wrote in his own language, all we get are translations.

But he contacted the Divine quite a bit and wrote over 40 books, his writings number 400 volumes and his lectures number over 600. This was someone who had something to say! And I put that down to having Neptune conjunct his Mercury.

He was a spokesperson for Neptune.

I meanwhile, I am feeling a bit of a failure.

I obviously have no idea what I'm talking about and at this moment I'm feeling considerably un-clever.

However, I've promised myself I'm going to continue this quest for 30 days and I've only just started.

Staying focused on what I want will surely allow me to connect in a way that suits me.

I'm sure the Divine is accommodating and considerate.

The fan is annoying me now.

I'm going to turn it off.

I can't sit here for much longer as dinner needs to be made and it won't get made with me contemplating my navel...

A dove is on the chimney pot above the fireplace and I can hear him/her cooing.

When I had my previous mystical experience I thought the birds were talking to me.

I could hear them chirping or calling or twittering and the sounds sounded like certain repetitive sequences of meaningful words.

Today I don't hear anything other than the bird.

I try and tune in for the first time in 30 years...

Ha, ha,

I just imagined that the bird said 'You're trying too hard'.

Ha

Maybe I am.

Maybe if I relax into this process it will be easier.

Onwards and upwards.

Day Three
Tuesday 30th July 19.30 2019
Went to Glastonbury today with our local group of therapists. Filled my water bottle with water from the Well. It's sitting in the kitchen now and I haven't decided what to do with it yet.

It was raining on and off while we were there. It's such a lovely place but all the signs asking for silence and quiet seemed pointless when someone next door was having some building work done and there were sounds of electric drills and blokes yelling.

I do seem to be more sensitive to noise at the moment.

After we'd had our trip and a cuppa I went to the Speaking Tree Bookshop. I could have spent hours in there just reading the titles of the books, never mind actually buying and reading the books themselves.

I bought three.

There were lots of books about spiritual happenings.

Advice on how to do it.

Where 'God' is located.

Bla Bla Bla.

I don't want to read about how *others* have done this.

I want to find out myself how to do it on my own.

Surely I don't need a primer or have to read a 'How To' book?

Wellesley Tudor Pole, the founder of the Chalice Well Trust was a Taurus, with Mercury and Neptune conjunct. There seems to be a theme going on here.

Name: ♂ Wellesley Tudor Pole
born on We., 23 April 1884
in Weston-Super-Mare, ENG (UK)
2w59, 51n21

Time: 6:00 a.m.
Univ.Time: 6:00
Sid. Time: 19:54:49

ASTRO)DIENST
www.astro.com

Type: 2.GW 0.0-1 5-Jun-2021

Natal Chart (Method: Web Style / Whole Signs)
Sun sign: Taurus
Ascendant: Taurus

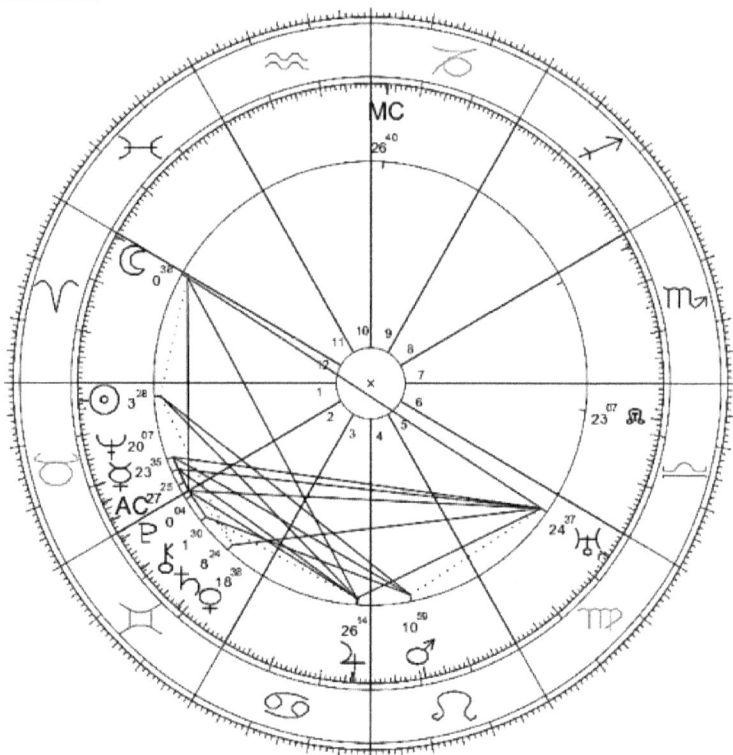

⊙ Sun	3 Tau 27'57"
☽ Moon	0 Ari 38' 4"
☿ Mercury	23 Tau 35'26"
♀ Venus	18 Gem 38'11"
♂ Mars	10 Leo 59'26"
♃ Jupiter	26 Can 14'24"
♄ Saturn	8 Gem 24'24"
♅ Uranus	24 Vir 37'23"r
♆ Neptune	20 Tau 6'32"
♇ Pluto	0 Gem 3'55"
☊ True Node	23 Lib 6'41"d
⚷ Chiron	1 Gem 29'30"

| AC: 27 Tau 24'42" | 2: 0 Gem 0' | 3: 0 Can 0' |
| MC: 26 Cap 40'16" | 11: 0 Pis 0' | 12: 0 Ari 0' |

22

I might not be contacting anything but I'm certainly doing the charts for people who have had a personal experience of this planet and have lived their lives expressing it.

When I was in the Chalice Well shop I saw a leaflet about the Lamplighter Movement but further investigations have drawn a blank. The original idea was from Tudor Pole who recommended lighting a candle at 9pm every night and the collective light would bring about peace. He also instigated the (Big Ben) Silent Minute which involved being silent for peace every night at 9pm.This tradition carried on from 1940 to somewhere in the 1960s

My experience was with light but as I've already said, I have no idea how I'd re-create that experience in a rational, everyday way.

There was nothing rational or everyday about the circumstances of my light experience.

Do only bonkers people get to experience the Divine?

Why can't membership of this exclusive club be open to ordinary, everyday folk?

It's raining again and looking very wet and dull outside my office.

I've got the fan on again but now I'm feeling a little chilly. But maybe that's not a bad thing because it will keep me awake and I feel rather tired.

How do everyday normal people connect with the Divine?

Is there any hope for us mere mortals?

On Thursday Mercury comes out of retrograde. It will be interesting to find out if that makes any difference with my attempts at Divine connection.

Maybe I'm expected to fast for a month.

Or pray continually for hours and hours.

Or would I have a better result if I sat in meditation in a certain position?

Why would I have to do these extreme things to get the connection I'd like to make?

I'm certainly not going to mess around with Ouija Boards or attempt anything wildly esoteric.

From my more than 30 years involvement in the spiritual/psychic movement, I know how all of that is definitely detrimental to mental health.

For sure.

I've seen far too many mentally wobbly people dabble in these things and find their lives get worse, not better.

I'd like to think that the Light I saw and the energy I experienced was a non-threatening and benign entity. That only wanted the best for me and now doesn't expect me to put myself in danger or stretch my brain cells.

Tomorrow is my day off and I've been invited to a funeral or 'celebration of life' for a little girl who was born as a Pisces with Sun conjunct Chiron, and Mercury conjunct Neptune. She was just over 3 years old and was born with a life-limiting condition.

She was a patient of mine, so is her mother.

That's three people in three days who have Mercury conjunct Neptune...

I've just checked my chart again and at this precise moment Neptune is conjunct my Sun and my Mercury.

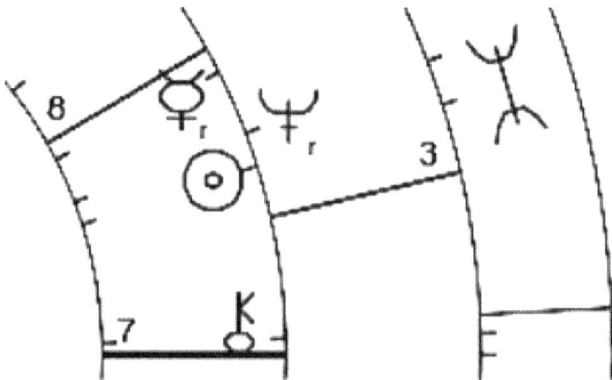

Hello.

Is anyone there?

Now I feel silly even writing that.

Of course whatever it is, is there.

It's always there.

It doesn't go anywhere.

It's us, the humans who ignore it or quite simply can't tune into it.

And I do think of it as being an 'it'.

My previous experience had nothing human about it at all.

It was just light.

Bright, white light.

Light I've never seen since.

And at this rate am never likely to see again.

Little Neriah's natal chart: Scorpio Ascendant, Sun in Pisces in the 5th house and Moon in Taurus in the 7th. Mercury conjunct Neptune in Pisces. Sun conjunct Chiron.

The planets on the outside of the chart are the date/time that she died: Scorpio Ascendant conjunct her natal Mars in Scorpio, retrograde transiting Jupiter conjunct her natal Saturn. Moon in Sagittarius = Mother has Moon in Sagittarius. Dad is a Scorpio. Transiting Saturn conjunct natal Pluto. Transiting Neptune conjunct natal Chiron. Transiting Uranus opposition Ascendant. She died suddenly with her parents holding her in love.

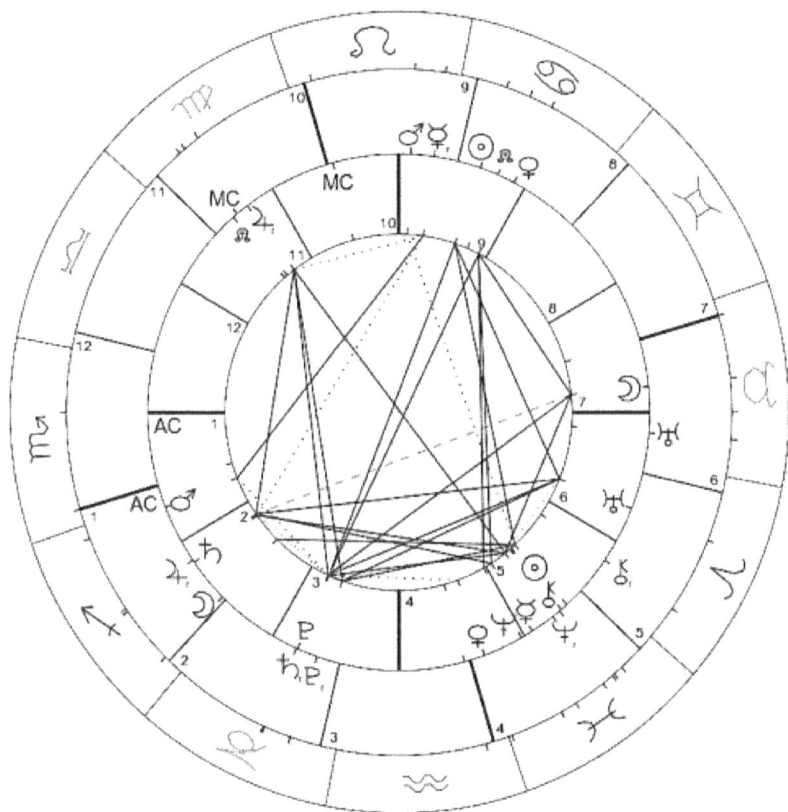

☉ Sun	22 Pis 47'16"	21 ♋ 57'
☽ Moon	16 Tau 31' 2"	26 ♐ 20'
☿ Mercury	12 Pis 55'50"	2 ♌ 46'r
♀ Venus	0 Pis 37'51"	13 ♋ 31'
♂ Mars	2 Sag 23'23"	8 ♌ 4'
♃ Jupiter	17 Vir 43'12"r	15 ♐ 41'r
♄ Saturn	16 Sag 16'31"	16 ♋ 51'r
♅ Uranus	18 Ari 53'39"	6 ♉ 17'
♆ Neptune	9 Pis 59'12"	18 ♓ 35'r
♇ Pluto	17 Cap 9'11"	21 ♑ 53'r
☊ True Node	21 Vir 47'14"	17 ♋ 39'd
⚷ Chiron	21 Pis 8'25"	5 ♈ 56'r

| AC: 10 Sco 50'49" | 2: 10 Sag 51' | 3: 10 Cap 51' | 27♏14' |
| MC: 25 Leo 52'56" | 11: 10 Vir 51' | 12: 10 Lib 51' | 20♍38' |

Day Four
Wednesday 31st July, 19.01

Went to the funeral reception today for the little Pisces girl. Her name was Neriah. Her name means 'Light of God'.

I made a little gift for her parents.

A small bottle of Chalice Well water, a hand-made handkerchief and the Astrology charts of Neriah's birth and remarkable time of death.

Both were under a Scorpio Ascendant.

Life

And Death.

Dad is also a Scorpio. Mum is a Gemini.

I went on my own and met a few people that I know from the choir...who I chatted with until they left. Then I chatted with people who seemed to also be on their own...one lady I was talking with was sat under a parasol. All of a sudden an enormous gust of wind caught the parasol and blew it over and 'crunch' I heard the sound of something breaking.

I closed my eyes and waited for the noise to stop, as I wasn't sure (as the parasol was behind me) what had happened. The parasol had flipped over a small hedge and the feet which had been held down by four concrete blocks, were all let loose and two large pottery flower pots had also all smashed on the concrete floor.

In seconds, members of waiting staff came over and took control of the situation and moved the parasol, restored the concrete blocks, and put back one pottery pot.

The other was smashed in half.

The friends of the lady I was talking with returned and seemed disappointed that they'd missed the excitement. I left them chatting and went to find the hosts to pay my respects and return home.

The Moon is in Leo now, a New Moon. As I have a Leo Ascendant, that does feel rather nice. Got annoyed a few moments ago as there was a very noisy fly in the room but it seems to have escaped. I didn't want to kill it so it must have gone into the hallway.

Good.

I've now closed the door.

I was thinking today that I really can't expect to have some dramatic experience with Neptune as

A) Neptune isn't the planet of dramatic happenings and

B) I need to look *under* what I'm involved in, as I'm sure I'll make some sense of it all at a later date.

Sometimes things make sense after they've happened, not while they occur.

Lovely and sunny now and I feel a little bad sitting here bashing out words when I could be sitting in the garden with our doglet in the sun.

I did dream this morning but I can't recall all the details.

If I don't write down my dreams the minute I wake up, they disappear and I'd feel strange sitting in bed scribbling down dreams.

I'd do it if I lived on my own but I don't.

I have to make an extra effort to remember them and today wasn't one of those days.

Mercury is now out of retrograde, which is a definite plus point.

Even though nothing dramatic is happening with Neptune, I do feel sort of tuned-into various nice things. I'm not battling anything at the moment. There seems to be a flow to what I'm writing and also what I'm doing in my work.

For years I'd worry about where-my-next-client-would-be-coming-from. Now I trust the Universe to allow people to find me.

It's a different approach.

As long as I'm discoverable, I'll be found.

I don't have to go overboard on self-promotion (although that comes naturally with my Fire Sign Ascendant!) and as I've been in private practice for more than 25 years, it comes much easier now.

Plus I haven't changed my job.

And I love what I do.

It has many facets and I love all of them.

Neptune.

Such a difficult planet to describe.

Even its discovery was shrouded in complexity, misinformation and international rivalry and discord.

I've realised after many years of observing it with my own chart and those of clients that too much Neptune causes confusion and bewilderment and not enough makes people materialistic and selfish.

There is a fine line between life and death and reality and illusion.

These are Neptune areas.

The sort of space between worlds.

The unseen.

The feeling you get when you go into a room and you realise someone has just had a row or an arguement.

You can feel the heavy energy in the air.

That's Neptune helping you sense things.

All of the human mechanisms for personal protection are destroyed though, by drugs.

You can feel other people's feelings, which is fine for a few minutes but can be totally exhausting after any length of time.

On this morning's dog walk the lady I was walking with was telling me how worried she was that her teen son would use drugs...then five minutes later she was telling me about how she's smoked what she thought was some cannabis at a festival but had felt so strange, she thought it had got mixed with something else.

I listened carefully in a totally non-judgmental way. She has to learn these things herself it's not my job.

Then I got home and as I'm writing this now, it seems appropriate for that discussion to happen while I am investigating Neptune.

Neptune can affect humans in the same way as cannabis.

Make you feel relaxed but paranoid.

Connected but apart.

De-motivated but full of ideas that will not go anywhere.

Too many people take drugs in the (mistaken) belief that in some way their thoughts/life will be better. The same goes for alcohol.

Maybe Neptune ought to be re-named as the God of Drugs!

But you can experience Neptune without having to imbibe loads of drink or drugs.

You can just allow yourself to *feel* more than normal.

Sense more than normal.

Trust your *body* to give you the signals you need to learn more about others and their intentions.

I was doing that today when I was at the celebration for the little girl.

Working out if me being with whoever I was with, was nice for them or annoying and when I sensed (as none of them knew me at all) they'd had enough I made an excuse to move on.

People's bodies always give them away too.

Body language must be THE most interesting subject ever, as all those subtle signals we give off, are easily understood by dogs or cats but us humans have to take classes to work it all out because our rational brains over-ride those signals.

Children know more than adults too.

And someone can make embarrassing pronouncements, when actually they're only saying it as it is.

Like the story of the Emperor Who Had No Clothes.

My youngest sister, who had Downs Syndrome and who I was very close to, was good at stating facts.

She once told a lady she worked with in the honey factory where they both worked, that she was fat.

She *was* fat

And Katy had spent her life watching her weight.

And she was only stating a fact.

She didn't say it to upset this lady (even though it did)

She'd said it because it was true and no amount of telling her not to say that sort of thing was going to work.

I was with my sister leading up to and when she died and the Ascending sign of Cancer was exactly on her natal Jupiter in the 6th.

I felt at that moment I had lost a large part of my family.

Transiting Moon in Virgo was on her natal Pluto, transiting Mars in Libra was conjunct her natal Mars, transiting Saturn was conjunct exactly her natal Neptune, transiting Uranus was also exactly conjunct her natal Moon and transiting Mercury retrograde was on her Ascendant.

She didn't go quietly.

She went loudly and with force.

Then it all went quiet.

I'd been holding her hand and my cousin was praying and the nurses were talking to her telling her I was with her...then just after she died, the wind chimes outside of her window sounded, as if a little breeze had passed over them.

But it was a totally windless day.

I thought that was her soul moving out of the window, flying high to wherever people go when they pass over.

I still miss her.

If I want to, I can connect with her but I know she's happy where she is because she's with our Mother, Father and brother and they're all together in heaven.

So, what's the point of Neptune?

What does it do for us that is good or positive?

How does it help us?

Lots of ways.

Ways we aren't conscious of.

If we are aware of it, it will help us live better, work better, be kinder to people and animals.

I don't understand how you could touch into the energies of Neptune, then eat a steak or kill something for dinner.

I was watching a ridiculous advert for M&S earlier.

They'd made a series of adverts for their 'market fresh range', or some other marketing ploy to make eating beef and piglets acceptable.

And I found the advert offensive (as I'm mostly vegan and I certainly don't eat meat.)

How could this farmer say he looked after his animals if he was going to send them to slaughter in a few months?

And the film had shots of pigs rolling in mud and wandering around a field but they didn't show footage of them screaming for their lives when they enter the slaughter house to get their throats slit or an electric stun gun aimed at their heads or suffocated with carbon dioxide. There is no escaping the fact that eating an animal involves employing someone to kill if for you. And those deaths are not needed. Humans can live very well on plants. (With a B12 supplement)

Increasing contact with Neptune does make you less likely to want anyone to suffer, let alone your dinner.

And that's where I'm at with this Neptune transit.

I've been Vegan since 2003.

I happily ate meat when I was younger. Our Mum went vegetarian when Katy was born but she cooked meat for all of us and our Dad. She never forced her eating habits on us.

And I did the same for my present husband and my son.

It's not my job to convert people to eating a plant-based diet.

It's my job to help people become aware of what they need to feel fulfilled in their lives, their way.

And Neptune certainly helps me in my work.

I can read a chart now and know exactly what the client needs to know to be who they'd like to be.

Which they might be already.

My connection with Neptune certainly feels as if it's there.

But my connection with the Divine doesn't.

And I'm not too sure how to reconcile that radical difference.

I live in hope.

Day Five

Thursday 1st August 21.22

Been working all this afternoon. Went to hygienist this morning and got stuck in loads of traffic.

This morning's dream stayed with me for a few minutes. Something about being with some people in a building and things weren't going the way I wanted them to.

I've had this dream a lot. Or variations of it.

I'm doing something or being somewhere and there's something wrong about it all. Either I'm in a shop working (previous work in reality) and my staff won't do what they're supposed to, or I do their job and things don't pan out how I'd like.

Or I'm in a building which is supposed to be my home, but it isn't because other people are in it and they don't belong there and I can't throw them out or remove them...how would I do that? I'm only five feet tall...

Or I'm travelling somewhere and I can't get to my destination because the train won't go along the lines I want.

All of these dreams repeat themselves and hardly change much.

Am I stuck somewhere in my spiritual development?

Do I even HAVE a spiritual destiny?

I do know this is something that people worry about as they get older.

I've read for people that as they get older, get more worried about their soul.

I'm not so worried about my soul, or even my soul purpose, I'm more concerned about this Neptune transit and am I making the best of it?

Am I working with it properly?

A lady I was working with this afternoon has natal Mercury conjunct Neptune.

That makes one a day now!!

Ha ha!

Maybe if I focus more on the present transiting Neptune conjunct my Mercury I'll feel better?

Get my message wherever it needs to go more easily?

Got to write my column tomorrow.

First thing in the morning, I'm doing the chart of the little girl who died for her mother. She said she'd like me to explain her chart (in English, Mum isn't an Astrologer) so she can understand that her life had meaning.

We all want to know that don't we?

That our lives and those of our children and family have meaning?

That those lives aren't pointless?

Mind you, I don't know many people whose lives are pointless. There is a point to most people's lives.

Maybe they can't see it themselves but it does exist.

I also know that younger people really stress about their first jobs and want to fall straight away into a wonderful, well paid, meaningful, important job...

Took me years to get to that place!

Certainly didn't expect it when I was starting out! In fact I almost took whatever work I was offered!

I don't have any concerns about my work, my job, my life-style, my friends, my partner or my family.

All of those things are tickitiboo

I'm sort of fretting about this Neptune thing and I suppose my biggest concern is this transit will finish in a few years, will never happen again in my life-time and I will have wasted Neptune's most wonderful blessings.

OK Mary, how likely is that to happen? That you waste this transit?

You're already working on finding the deeper meaning to this planet aren't you?

Well, Yes I am and I hope I'm doing it in the right way.

I think I'd like some sort of a sign that this is OK for me to do it?

And what sort of sign would I want?

Writing in the sky?

Get real, things like that don't happen.

Just stay focused on being open to whatever blessings Neptune brings in all his Water God-ness.

OK

I think I can do that.

I'll stay open and alert to possibilities.

Fighting myself during this Mars-in-Leo transit won't help. Got cross about a person who isn't a client, her mother is, this morning and had to force myself to read her email reply before I even had breakfast as I might have got indigestion if I'd read it while I ate.

At one point I wanted to phone my supervisor and ask her to stay on the line while I read the email. I was sort of floundering about the dilemma.

In the end I opened the email and it wasn't as bad as I'd worried about all night.

I'm not replying again.

I've already explained my reasoning and my reasons for my reply. Move on...

I'm not the only astrologer in the world! There are plenty out there and I'm not the right fit for this person.

All of that took a lot of my personal energies...

I will chat it through with my supervisor next time I see her.

It's a problem a lot of therapists face. I hadn't had it for quite a few years.

I have terms and conditions bla bla bla but it's almost as if people don't read them or understand them properly.

My son had a similar problem himself today and we discussed Terms and Conditions by text.

Sigh

I'm a bit late with my writing today and it's past my bedtime.

Another day tomorrow.

Day Six

Friday 2nd August, 20.59

Met up with the Mum & Dad of little Pisces girlie. Explained their child's chart to them so they could understand how, even though she as born with a syndrome, it didn't detract from her wonderful energy that touched so many people.

Then I noticed Mum has Moon conjunct Neptune...

I do seem to be working with and coming across far more people than 'normal' who have a Neptune signature. And so it should be as I'm spending these 30 days focusing on this particular planet.

Went to a second-hand bookshop after the meeting. A lot of times I find books help me when I have questions or am feeling unsure about something. I like to read books by people who have done what I would like to do, or who have experienced something I am interested in.

One of the books will have to go back to a charity shop as I found out the birth data of the author and I really don't want to be reading a book written by someone with Sun conjunct Pluto and Moon in Scorpio.

That won't work with me today.

I rarely read fiction unless it's written by my sister! Or are fairytales. Even then I prefer to stick to non-fiction to keep my brain firmly on planet Earth. As a Pisces my life-lesson is to learn to be practical and not be away with those pesky fairies.

Just realised I haven't written my Newsletter for this month.

Sigh.

Will have to do it tomorrow and also write the following month's column for the local free magazine.

I've been writing an editorial Astrology column for almost 15 years now.

I've written one for my Newsletter since the late 1990s.

Every month, paying attention to the transits for each sign of the Zodiac.

I like transits.

I like the way they don't last forever, so if something horrible or upsetting is happening, depending on the transit, I can calculate how long it will last.

This too soon will pass.

It's a natural human reaction to stress to want it to end NOW.

However, when an understanding is gained about the planet concerned and that the 'horrible happening' might be part of your soul-purpose, it can certainly help people feel better.

That it won't last forever.

Things will improve....

Those are all nice things to hear when you're stressed.

It gives hope.

When there is more understanding about life and spirituality, stressful moments can become teachings or learnings.

They can help us grow.

Possibly.

Or not.

Depending on the person.

I'm feeling a little better about my little project I've set myself, to 'be aware' of Neptune.

I know it's not the sort of planet to respond at all well to being forced, or commanded, or even pleaded with.

It'll do whatever it has to do in a way that can't be described so easily with words.

Some artists and poets tune into Neptune.

They let the 'Art' flow through them.

Fellow Pisces author Julia Cameron talks about getting out of the way and letting 'God' come though.

I'm opening myself to this too.

This morning's dream was all about shit.

Not something I'm happy about writing about. Spent time with my journal analysing what the dream meant and it is something along the lines of there I am, trying to get my shit together and I feel as if I'm doing it in public, which really doesn't gel for me.

That's a private thing.

Maybe this exercise needs to stay private and not be shared.

At the moment all I'm bothered about is making sure I stay focused on Neptune and allow myself to be bathed by its beauty.

Because it is a beautiful planet.

It's blue.

I have no idea what it looks like through a telescope because I've never seen it myself. Only read about it.

And it's certainly not visible to the naked eye and wasn't discovered until telescopes were invented.

And even though they were invented that's not how it was discovered. That was done by mathematical calculation and a desire to find out why Uranus' orbit was so wobbly.

I know all the history.

I've studied it.

I teach it to my Astrology students.

Neptune's discovery was a mysterious event.

And isn't that how Neptune operates now?

With mystery?

Those intuitive moments that are so fleeting but meaningful.

That's a Neptune moment.

Something that brings awe but also confusion.

What would Neptune want us on Earth to know or experience?

Surely it would want us to know we are not separate?

That we are part of something way, way bigger.

And that we are all connected in some way.

Something like that happened a few hours ago when I recommended an Astrologer to someone in the USA who *already knew* that Astrologer!

I didn't know that.

I only knew this Astrologer is a member of the same organisation as me and lives near to where this client lives. There are plenty in the area but I hit on one that I thought they might like and found out just now that my client had already worked with them!

Win, win!

My Gemini Auntie, who loved Astrology, used to collect co-incidences.

She loved hearing about random things happening, that turned out couldn't be random at all.

My first boyfriend and I met at a party in a queue on the stairs for the one loo in the house.

We got chatting, as he was just ahead of me in the queue and we discovered we had the exact same birthday (different years)

We then spent the rest of the party telling people we were twins!

We were together for 5 years.

I was devastated when the relationship ended.

Sun in the 7th

I found out on the first night my present husband and I met, that his ex-wife has the same birthday as me... different year.

And just to make it even more weird.

My son dated a girl whose mother has the exact same birthday as me and same year too!

Bonkers!

These were the sort of things my Auntie collected.

She just loved a good co-incidence.

And most people have had them.

Which takes me back to the fact that we are all connected in some way if we care to investigate the connections a little more.

Day Seven

Saturday 3rd August 20.04

Hubbie let me lie in while he took doglet for a walk and I managed to wake from a dream.

I was indoors. It wasn't my house. I was with people I didn't really like. Can't remember much else or what the point of the dream was.

Had a client first thing this morning. Felt really bad after the reading when I realised they'd booked 90 mins and I'd only been with them for 70 mins.

Emailed a discount code and lots of written info about their chart and links to my Hypno Tracks.

Felt as if I'd short changed them, which is a terrible feeling.

I did check before I said goodbye if I'd answered all their questions or if there was anything else they wanted to cover.

Haven't heard back so I don't know if they hate me or not.

Decided to read the book I thought I wouldn't like. Skipping through it a bit so I can get the gist of it.

Rather on the wordy side. Spending three or more pages saying something that could have been said in a few words but it was written quite a while ago and that was the 'fashion' then.

The publisher was a client of mine, which was part of the attraction to me buying it, and the title seemed helpful after speaking with the grieving Mum and Dad.

I tend to read more than one book at a time. I have books in certain rooms and always one in the bedroom or my Kindle so at least I have something to read before I sleep.

Sleep is SO important for a Pisces. And dreaming quenches a spiritual thirst, except my dreams are frustrating and stupid at the moment.

Not feeling very good about myself this evening.

Done some nice home cooking but I feel useless and I don't seem to have got this Neptune thing in the bag.

It's one week now since I started and I don't feel I have much to show for it.

I wonder who is that who is talking to me like that?

What part of me?

My Leo Ascendant?

The bit that needs recognition, praise, applause, prizes...lots of "Well Done"

Sigh

My Sun is in the 7th and it's all about relationships.

And enemies.

Had enough of them over the years. Sceptics bent on making my life hell because I'm trained in Homeopathy.

Haven't been very far today either. Popped to Post Office to post a package to a client. Stood in the queue and watched lady with white, bleached hair get frustrated as she was learning on the job and her co-worker was talking her through how to do each transaction.

I could see that she was getting flustered. And maybe not really taking everything in that was happening, as there were lots of tasks she had to complete to help each person.

My package caused a bit of a fuss because I said it contained a 'Flower Essence' when it fact it contained a Homeopathic remedy.

But you try explaining that to a Post Office employee.

It isn't on their list.

Training co-worker said 'Oh, that's perfume' ready to ban my package but I quickly replied that it wasn't anything to do with perfume.

The package contained a small bottle of water and alcohol, less than 4cm high, which is called Tempesta and is made from a thunderstorm.

The story would have been far too long to explain even to you and this writing isn't an account of Homeopathic remedies so just believe me when I say the remedy helps attract a soul-mate and we'll leave it at that.

Job done.

Training co-worker made a comment about package needing my address on '*in case customs wants to return item*' which was almost as if she'd cursed my package and wanted it not to be safe enough to send overseas.

Sigh again.

Checked my chart again to find out what's happening today.

I keep forgetting I'm having my second Saturn Return.

I have already planned for that, so that's not an issue.

Mars on my Ascendant probably isn't helping.

I'll have to go for a long dog walk tomorrow to jiggle that Mars. Release the energy as Mars represents Action, Aggression and Energy. And all I'm feeling is mild anger and dissatisfaction.

Which is silly really as I have heaps to be grateful for.

I suppose I'm not feeling very creative and that's always a death knell for me.

I have to feel as if I'm involved in something wonderful, amazing or creative in some way.

I come from a family of creative people.

Writing helps.

Having something exciting helps even more.

Maybe I'm an excitement junkie?

Moon is in Virgo conjuncting my natal Pluto in the first house.

I cleaned the kitchen floor earlier and that felt good.

And I've completely organised all my health issues. Could do with lowering my blood sugars a bit as if they go too high I'm no good to anyone.

Excitement junkie.

I need to have something exciting to look forward to, or to be involved in.

And with retirement looming I'm worrying all that will end the minute I stop being a therapist.

But I don't want to be a therapist anymore.

20+ years of helping people with their health issues. I want to help my *own* health now and even writing that seems selfish..

Third sigh.

I can do Astrology anywhere.

On a desert island, on a plane, train, and/or in a car.

Online, in person, by letter, email, message, any form of social media. I've got so many ways of working with people. No shortage.

I could probably do it in my sleep.

But healing people's health issues.

I've reached a clear expiration date: 31st December 2019.

My new year will start without having to use The Repertory (book of symptoms), choose remedies, work out rubrics, deal with aggravations or all the other things a homeopath has to deal with to help a client.

It's a long, time-consuming process and I've loved it for years and years and now I've had enough.

My practice began with a dying client and has ended with a child dying.

That's my Pluto talking and I seem to be ignoring it in my quest to listen to Neptune.

OK Pluto, thank you for your obsessive help over the years and for the enthusiasm to be a healer. I would like to take my Homeopathic retirement soon though.

Is that OK with you?

I can use all those skills in my Astrology practice and I've passed on my clients to a younger person. Keeping the light shining in the same way as when I started: an older Homeopath gave me all her books on Astrology, as she'd decide to retire from Astrology and concentrate on her Homeopathy.

And my supervisor has also retired.

I'm ten years younger than her.

I'm now nearly the age she was when she retired her practice.

Moon on my Pluto is asking me how I actually *feel* about not being a healer anymore.

How do I feel?

One part of me feels a deep sorrow.

The other part of me feels relief.

It was the same when my youngest sister died.

I was bereft.

The grief was massive.

And I also felt relief that she wasn't suffering anymore and neither was I, because her illness and untimely death was a 24-hour worry for me. I ran her care package and spent so much time with her.

Now she's released from that suffering and that was something my lovely son reminded me of.

That death is an end of suffering.

(*Assuming of course that the person is suffering*)

The book I'm reading is all about death.

The dirty secret.

That's Pluto territory and I suppose I have to pass through that a bit before I can allow Neptune to leak through.

Transiting Pluto is also on my natal Saturn, so I'm not only having a Saturn return, I'm also having a Pluto Meets Saturn Event. And all of that is happening in my 5th house of creativity.

No wonder I don't feel very creative at the moment or fluffy.

There's a war going on and I'm trying to avoid it.

The three outer planets are in Water and Earth.

Uranus in Taurus

Neptune in Pisces

Pluto in Capricorn

None of those are causing awful aspects to any of my natal planets.

Apart from the conjunction, Pluto isn't squaring as I have no planets in Aries or Libra.

Feel like my blood sugars have dropped as I feel hot and sweaty for no reason.

Will have to blood test and sort myself out.

Day Ten

Tuesday 6th August 10.03

Feel bad that I've skipped two days with no good excuse. Cloudy today. Sort of feels ominous, as if a big storm is on its way.

Neptune is now 18 degrees Pisces and is retrograding over my Sun and Mercury and will continue retrograding until the end of November. It does feel as if my life energies are slipping away and it's not a nice feeling. Why do I have to experience the negative side of Neptune? Surely I should feel it more acutely while it retrogrades?

It does feel sadder.

A friend of mine's husband is terminally ill. He's a really nice chap and getting the diagnosis must have been devastating when he'd already recovered from cancer in another area of the body.

Dying isn't very fashionable and you're at the mercy of 'consultants' and 'experts' and 'oncologists'.

All these people having an input into treatment and life expectancy.

But how much do these people know about him as a person?

In fact I've got two friends who are living with cancer at the moment.

The other person was told by their oncologist that there was 'nothing they could do'.

What an awful thing to say to someone about anything.

Implying that they're not going to support you....awful...

The War on Cancer certainly hasn't been won by anyone... that's what killed my Dad and my brother. They both died of the same thing at the same age: bowel cancer.

This morning's dream was all about being in a building and having to make a journey, a long journey to two different places I'd never visited before.

I knew that the person I'd just met had made this journey but I hadn't and I just didn't know how to get there.

I had a car.

I think it had a Sat Nav.

I knew I had to go up the map.

I was trying to get hold of them and speak to them so I could get some directions.

Now I'm thinking about it, was the dream telling me I need to contact my friend and her husband and ask them how they are? (We haven't spoken for a few weeks)

Is the journey they're making the same as the one we'll all have to make?

To death?

Will have to check my diary and see if there was anything else in that dream that might help.

I got up earlier today so I can get some things done. I've already written my column and my Newsletter is poised to go.

I wonder about my writing and if it's helpful for/to anyone.

Writing sometimes feels like shouting very loudly into a void and wondering if anyone will hear the echoes.

I do know now though, after writing a number of books, that the best writing is done when the writing itself isn't self-conscious. When the words just hit the page.

Editing happens later.

Words need to spew first.

Neptune.

Are you helping me?

Are you helping anyone?

I wonder if it's possible to just focus on one planet when there are 10 that Astrologers use in our Solar System, including, obviously, The Sun, the Life Giving Planet. As without it we are all dead...

Can I ignore Pluto in Capricorn and Saturn in Capricorn and just listen to what Neptune wants us to know?

I do know that floods and storms are Neptune's territory and there's a piece in the news at the moment about a dam in Whaley Bridge south of Manchester that's been damaged in a storm. I follow a cake-making business on Facebook and the owners live in this town and for two or three days have been posting on their page apologies for not being able to mail out cakes because they've been evacuated from their business.

Water has a life of its own and the more we mess with it and try and re-direct from where it wants to go, the worse things will be.

The Sun has just briefly appeared from behind a cloud.

Maybe that's the message that Neptune wants us to learn during this transit, that water must be respected far, far more.

Since Neptune entered Pisces the numbers of people drowning at sea has reached unprecedented levels.

Homeless.

Desperate.

Asylum seekers.

I had a client who volunteered a number of times to help the people washed up in Greece. He met the boats and gave the rescued people warm dry clothes. Helped them reach land and safety. But his help was such a small drop in the ocean, literally. He wasn't part of any organisation and sort of helped them on a whim to 'do good'. But he got overwhelmed and returned.

It isn't any good helping others when your own life is a mess and his was.

It's not the physical-ness of it that was wearing.

It was the emotional component.

And I know all about that.

I can't help my clients if I'm a wobbly mess (which I'm not at the moment)

I have been in the past.

I suppose Neptune, even though it dissolves boundaries, allows us to merge with others but lose our own definition.

And too much Neptune sends us to places that can suffocate and drown us.

Literally.

Chapter Two

Starting to Be Neptune-d

Day 12

Thursday 8th August, 21.34

Missed another day. This is Neptune stuff for sure.

Getting slack.

Letting things slide.

Losing focus.

Allowing distractions to interfere...

Long and complicated dream this morning about being 'at work' with someone who was a counsellor.

I can't remember the full gist of the dream but I'll write it in later...

I had a baby girl in a buggy. She was mine. Then she went missing. I wasn't fazed. I was more concerned about getting in the lift and getting to my destination.

Another client with Mercury conjunct Neptune. Told them they had the same chart as Rudolph Steiner (which they do have).

Memory is suffering. Finding it harder than usual to remember simple things like names of places or even things.

I know I have pernicious anaemia and it can mean when my next jab is due, my memory goes AWOL, but this is worse then normal and I've only just got topped up...

Moon is in Sagittarius now opposite my natal Moon. Generally an optimistic Moon sign to transit.

Weather warnings about wind. Not mad on wind. Can't ride my motor scooter in wind. Far too dangerous.

Quite a few weather warnings in the U.K at the moment and it's now much wetter than normal for this time of year. This is supposed to be our Summer!

Definitely picking up people's moods more easily too.

Not so much their thoughts but finding body language far easier to interpret. And also reading between the lines. Understanding what people *really* mean when they talk to or with me.

That's nice.

I'm enjoying that aspect of this transit.

Just don't like the memory issues.

I can hear the rain outside.

Hear the traffic travelling through the rain. Makes the cars sound swishier, when this time of night I'd never hear a car go past. With the rain I hear the swish of the wet road and the tyres.

I can also tell when people are lying.

I could do that reasonably well anyway, but now I can radar into the 'truth' of what is being said.

Spent all of this morning with a hypnotherapy client.

Then the afternoon with my bestie friends. That was fab.

If I didn't have to do anything, I'd happily spend all day reading books.

I could quite easily just sit somewhere comfortable with our doglet and a good book and just read.

Lots.

Working on reducing my homeopathy practice and resurrecting my previous business which was called Future Path.

I liked the name when I first used it in the 1990s

And I'm happy to use it again.

I don't actually run a business anyway, I'm a sole trader but I need to have something to write on invoices and my name doesn't describe what I do.

The Moon will be meeting up with Jupiter while the Sun is conjuncting transiting Venus. Strange combo but all in Fire signs.

Will have to set myself a reminder to write tomorrow and not forget, but since I'll be spending most of the day with clients overseas that won't be hard because my computer screen will already be in front of me.

I sort of feel like I'm going backwards. As if I am stuck on a barge getting pushed back along the canal by the force of the water.

We walked along by the canal tonight and I thought how much I liked doing that and how I'd missed doing it but didn't miss it until I realised how nice it was.

There's something deeply emotional about walking by water.

Bridges.

Barges.

Canal boats.

Ducks and swans...and the water just moving in a watery type of way...soothing to the soul.

Generally the local canal and river are gentle but I expect with this weather warning it will totally change.

Glad I don't live on there! And lots of people do in Bath!

Day 13

Friday 9th August 20.33

I had been pondering stopping writing until Neptune comes out of retrograde on the 28th of November but just after I'd written that my Word crashed and didn't save what I'd written...so I think I'll take that as a sign that that is not what's needed now.

And when we do get to the end of November, Neptune will be exactly conjunct my Sun, again.

Last little sweep for the next couple of hundred years...

Weather reports are all predicting 'dreadful' storms tomorrow with lots of wind and rain.

Fast wind.

50-60mph

I wonder sometimes how accurate weather reports are.

Two festivals have been cancelled, one of which my son was travelling to attend, so was the daughter of a friend.

This doesn't seem that 'normal' for this time of year.

Usually, the U.K. has its 'best' weather in August, hence it being one of the months allotted for school holidays.

'Unseasonably wet and windy weather on its way' says the B.B.C. weather site.

Now I'm not *blaming* this on Neptune, I'm just pointing out that this is typical Neptune territory.

That and lies and illusion and delusion...or on a more positive spin: Spirituality and Sublime Connection.

That's where I'm placing my focus, on the spirituality.

The big disadvantage of connecting with any version of spirituality, is it completely removes a person from *also* connecting with reality.

And I'd like to know if it's possible to do both.

I *might* be able to, as Saturn is in Capricorn, my birth combination and Saturn's happy home. OK I'm having a Saturn return but I do have a good relationship with Saturn.

And if I keep hold of (mentally) that Saturn energy I'm much less likely to drift away with whatever Neptune is all about.

I don't want a struggle with this.

I want flow.

In my work I do speak with a lot of people who are either trying to 'find' themselves, or are seeking spiritual guidance. But what advice can you give people in that situation?

Pray?

But who is going to pray when they don't believe in God?

And how will praying help anyway?

I'm not attempting to connect with anything as vast and expansive as a god. Neptune is a planet not a god.

If as an Astrologer I believe that the planets add meaning to our lives, then what meaning am I attributing to this planet?

And why am I even attributing a meaning to it?

Everything I've ever learned about Astrology I've learned from books, written by other people.

Am I just spouting words I've learned?

What is *my* actual experience of Astrology?

I can barely make out planets in the sky other than the Sun and the Moon.

Jupiter is easy enough...

I've never witnessed Mercury and have a few times seen Venus and Mars.

But I've never seen any of the other planets and certainly not Neptune, Uranus or Pluto.

I have to place my trust in that what I've read and other people have experienced and studied is correct.

I have no reason to *not* believe them.

Have I?

Why is Astrology so compelling? (for me)

I suppose I can answer some of those questions with a Why Not?

Is it all fantasy?

But isn't that what Neptune is all about?

When you study Astrology deeply you realise, well I have, that all of life is expressed in it.

Unlike Astronomy which is all about weights and speeds and distances (and no emotion and few adjectives)

Astrology is about the *human* experience.

Astrology makes us understand each other better.

I understand you because I know your chart.

And I also know the major significance of Neptune transiting through the sign that it has an affinity with and I'm still astounded that so few people, (astrologers included) are writing about it!

This is a once in a lifetime occurrence.

Like when Pluto transited through the sign of Scorpio in the 1980s

Or Uranus transited through Aquarius in 2000s

And now while Jupiter transits through Sagittarius and Saturn through Capricorn.

All of these are planets transiting through the signs they have the best relationship with.

It's like wearing the right clothes to the party.

Or having a brolly in rainy weather.

Or sunglasses on a bright day.

I've lived so far in my life with ruling planets going through their home-y signs and these planetary transits won't happen again for a long, long time.

Isn't that something to celebrate?

Enjoy?

Talk about?

Write about?

I suppose these days we're so easily distracted but I refuse to be distracted from this happening.

I'm just a very short, getting elderly, Pisces female, asking for a planet to let me know what it wants 'us' to know.

And maybe it doesn't want us to know anything.

Maybe it's perfectly happy where it is, doing what it's doing, far away in deep space.

But if I also take into account the belief that we are all connected, not just as humans but to other living and non-living beings. Then surely Neptune might want to let a few of us on planet Earth know about what its like to be a planet, deep in space, never coming across anything other than cosmic wind?

Maybe it does sense that 'we' are over here, just as we, possibly, can do that from Earth. By using scientific equipment and the famous mathematical equations that discovered its existence because for thousands of years we never even knew Neptune existed.

Maybe previous generations didn't need to know about its existence.

And maybe we do now, because we're poisoning our planet and destroying our world.

Maybe Neptune wants us to know that we only have one chance at life. It won't happen again if we destroy our Earth.

There isn't another Earth.

Maybe Neptune wants us to know what it feels like to once have been a planet with life and now to be cold and orbiting ceaselessly and unproductively around the Sun and possibly a few other Suns in other galaxies.

Maybe it wants us to know we don't have to destroy our planet and we can live without using up all the worldly resources. That people like Greta Thunberg are saying what needs to be said and having to repeat, repeat, repeat that it *is* a climate emergency and our house *is* burning down and unless we unite a teeny bit with each other, that's it.

No planet earth

Ever.

Is that the message?

Are we listening?

Who is speaking Neptune's message most clearly?

It has to be someone who isn't doing it for the money or the fame or the Facebook likes.

People like Greta or Charles Eisenstein.

Just naming two I can think of at the moment.

It's not even about Peace.

That's Venus' realm.

It's about connecting with that which is more beautiful, more wondrous, more gasp-making and loss-for-words.

That feeling of connecting with everything that matters.

Everything.

Life the Universe and Everything.

People can get into that state when they've had too much to drink or imbibed various mind-altering substances.

But I'm stone cold sober and its late and I don't even have a glass of water with me at the moment because even that would take me away from the page, as I try to tune into what Neptune wants us to know and I have no idea if I'm even 1% near to that.

It's tear-making.

I feel tearful.

I just feel sadness that maybe we aren't listening and it's all too late and Neptune has been in this sign before and we didn't listen then and why would we even listen now? But maybe he/she /it, is trying again because wouldn't it be wonderful if we *did* listen?

To our hearts or even better to our collective, unconscious hearts?

Maybe being tearful is the only way to connect.

Being happy and smiley won't do it.

Over the last few weeks a little girl has died and another client's partner died in the shower. Today I was counselling her (because her counsellor is away) as she was stressing about the autopsy report she had read, thinking she'd neglected her partner because he'd had one of her painkillers for his backache...

But she'd heard him fall in the bathroom and she went to find him. He had collapsed and she performed Cardiopulmonary resuscitation, C.P.R. on him and kept him alive until the paramedics arrived.

Lord knows how she rang for an ambulance *and* carried on with the C.P.R. but she did.

And she's blaming herself because she would have cared for him but his family made the decision to turn off his life-support...

And all of this was sadder than sad.

Maybe it's only with tears and a sense of loss that we can experience Neptune's message right now.

Tears...

16th August 11.02am

I seem to be getting slack. Not paying attention to this writing. Easily distracted.

In my defence I do work from home, which although it gives a wonderful sense of freedom to do whatever I want, I could starve if I didn't see clients or do things other than write.

And writing is almost a thankless task.

It takes years to realise that the only person you're pleasing when you write, is yourself. If no one reads what you write, then you have to like what you've written.

A weird sort of juggling act.

Still coming across lots of clients with Neptune issues.

Maybe as I'm so tuned into Neptune at the moment, I'm attracting clients equally involved, unconsciously.

I've re-vitalised my Hypnotherapy practice, as that's where the real work needs to happen to truly understand this planet.

It's not the conscious part of ourselves, like the Sun is.

Or even the emotional subconscious, like the Moon... it's further than that.

The Collective Unconscious.

My dreams are your dreams are everyone's dreams.

It was 50 years after the discovery of Neptune in 1846, that Sigmund Freud in 1896 named his therapy Psychoanalysis.

He was born in 1856 ten years after Neptune was discovered, so you could say he spent most of his life exploring the planet, on Earth, by exploring people's minds.

Their unconscious minds.

And he was another person born while Neptune was transiting through the sign of Pisces, like it is now.

Will there be the same inspiration to investigate how we observe the world?

He was also born when Uranus was in Taurus, (conjunct his Sun) and Uranus is presently transiting through Taurus right now.

Just checked...

His theories of Psychoanalysis were 'invented' during a Neptune transit! Neptune was conjunct his natal Mercury when he coined the term and had already spent a number of years transiting his Sun sign.

He started out in practice using Hypnosis, but then opted for 'free association' allowing/encouraging his client to just talk about whatever came to them to help release suppressed memories and/or emotions.

What would happen if I just 'allowed' a few more things to happen, without trying to control things so much?

How would that be?

Just intuited them?

What would happen?

No idea what day I am now, but it's...

22nd August 11.20am

Ha!

That's Neptune country! Having no idea what something is and losing track of time. I can certainly work it out and subtract one from another, but I sort of feel what's the point.

My private practice has suddenly gone awfully quiet. It does this every now and then. Either I've taken my eye off the ball, or everyone-and-his-wife are on holiday.

I used to completely freak out when my business went quiet, now I don't. I just get on and do other things associated with it, like filing, or writing...

You can't work AND write! Writing IS work.

And keeping track of Neptune is very interesting.

I've never done it before...I am enjoying it. Having this enormous awareness of a planet's 'voice' and 'story'.

I've just been sent a chart from a podcast-listener of his boyfriend and the chart has Sun conjunct Mars, Venus, Mercury, Uranus and Neptune.

There we have a wonderful example of someone being born with a whole cluster of planets conjunct Neptune.

Blimey!

I haven't heard back from them yet, as they're in the USA and they won't be out of bed yet.

Both of them, him and his boyfriend, were born during the Uranus/Neptune conjunction on the 1990s

This was a once-in-lots-of-lifetimes event and I wrote about it in my book *The Astrology of Indigos, Everyday Solutions to Spiritual Difficulties.*

This 'Indigo' generation is now having Saturn transiting over their Uranus/Neptune natal conjunction, so they're taking seriously things like Astrology and natural alternatives.

They're also experiencing a rather dramatic awakening...

When a mid-planet like Saturn or Jupiter crosses over a natal outer planet: Uranus, Neptune and Pluto and does it for the first time, all sorts of weird s*** happens.

Or the other way, Uranus, Neptune or Pluto crossing natal Jupiter or Saturn.

These are times when whatever does happen, is telling a story of something bigger than the self.

I was 21 when transiting Neptune became conjunct to my natal Jupiter. It had spent the previous year getting closer and by the time I actually hit 21, I was away with the fairies.

Luckily I came back with a bump and I'm still here.

So I understand the angst associated with having 'an awakening' and depending on which planet is involved, will determine how that plays out in your life.

Some people, obviously, never have them. Other are *so* sensitive to planetary energies that all it takes is the Moon to change sign, and they're feeling it.

Luckily, I'm not that bad!

This is a long transit with Neptune and after it finishes it will never return in my chart.

It will also never conjunct again any natal planet of mine unless I live to be very old.

That's it.

In a few years the cycle will be all gone... I'll have to live to 95 for it to conjunct my natal Moon in Gemini.

And Lord knows if that will ever happen and would I want to live that long?

I'd have to live through Pluto being in Pisces, my Sun sign and having a Uranus return.

In 10 years time I'll have to cope with Uranus making a conjunction to my Moon, which I've never experienced before, so there's still quite a lot of transiting aspects I've never felt before and don't know if I will...so I'm making the best of *this* transit.

And paying attention to what Neptune wants me to know.

On the one hand spirituality seems a super answer to life's questions.

But on the other it doesn't make a blind bit of difference to the world's everyday life.

When you look back through history, not one religious movement did any 'good' to the Earth or it's people. In fact you could say all it did was make us go to war against each other because each side thought they were the enlightened ones and the other side were non-believers therefore they needed to be eradicated.

That's a sad thought.

That someone's personal enlightenment brings about the destruction of other, living beings because of a disagreement about who is 'right'.

It happened then and it still happens now.

I wonder sometimes if whatever consciousness a planet has, it looks at us here on Earth and wonders: "What the hell are they doing over there?"

"They've got light, water and plants, which we on our dead little planet don't have, and they're fighting and destroying not only each other in wars, but also ruining the resources, burning them, digging them up, polluting the air, wasting so much...for what? Money? What's money when you have everything?"

And it's hard to reconcile those thoughts.

One about the wonderfulness of life.

And the other about bills and drudgery...

Is there a way to live *between* each of those thoughts?

In a sort of in-betweeny state?

Not hating?

Not fighting?

Having acceptance for whatever is, or happens?

Planets certainly don't fight with each other.

They just orbit, orbit, orbit...

And Neptune possibly urges us to remember it doesn't have to be this way.

We can touch into different dimensions and use them to bolster us while we suffer.

Thursday 5th September 2.40pm

Now I'm feeling *really* bad because I haven't written for days.

Reached the stage where I feel what I'm doing is totally useless, which is a dreadful feeling.

Neptune is advancing his transit and all I seem to be able to do it scroll through my social media stream and service clients. I even told my son yesterday my writing had come to a stop.

:(

Started reading Rudolph Steiner's *How to Know Higher Worlds*...and I'm even struggling with the title and the use of the words 'Higher' as if contacting or communicating with something outside our daily experience is higher...than? What?

Is everyone else on a lower plane or world?

Is Earth a 'lower' place.

However, I also totally appreciate that writing about these subjects means we don't actually have the relevant words in our 'everyday' vocabulary.

Also Rudolph lived during the end of the last Neptune transit, which started in 1849.

Which feels a little weird.

If he wasn't a physical manifestation of this planet, I don't know who is!

11th Sept 14.01

Got a typical Neptune symptom. Feeling as if my brain is swimming. Dizzy and very unsteady. Waiting for the doctor's receptionist to answer the phone.

I'm caller number 5.."please hold"...now I'm 4...now I'm 3 in the queue "please hold".

Head is swimming.

Not feeling good at all.

Thinking is a struggle.

Luckily I don't have any clients until next week now.

Don't think I could read at the moment.

20th September 10.56am

Moved on a little now. Dizziness was due to low iron. Have upped my intake and am back to normal now.

Today's realisation was I don't need to look outside of myself for these answers I'm searching for...I just need to, and I use that word 'just' gently, give myself some time.

So today, I've started a meditation ritual. Only 5 minutes and straight after waking up. Sat up in the bed and managed 3 mins before I glanced at the clock.

Today is a Universal Strike for Climate and I can't make the meeting at the Guildhall in Bath because I have a client at 11am this morning.

Scribbling these words to express that connection with the divine and Neptune is all about *not* doing things, *not* wanting, *not* searching...just being.

Sounds so lovely and easy but can I commit to the practice?

My impatient Leo Ascendant wants it all NOW.

Maybe I do have it now and I just haven't recognised it.

Maybe I do have everything I need right now for this moment.

Client is a tad late.

I know she has trouble getting up in the morning as Pisces can and do.

I'll give her another 5-10 mins then I'll have to cancel her.

I can spend that time writing to you, communicating with you. Because I know you're there and you only want the best for me.

For everyone in fact.

Read Steiner's book about Higher Worlds.

...gotta dash client has arrived...feeling pleased with myself that I managed 5 mins meditation though.

14.07

Lovely sunny day today. ..

Carrying on from earlier...

Neptune is definitely making himself known today with the Climate Strike. Lots of people out in the sun, all marching to protest and make politicians know that it's time for platitudes to end.

No more words.

Action is what's needed.

If nothing else, at least people are far more aware of the climate.

I don't remember anything as big as this happening world-wide.

It's as if Neptune is now having his voice heard, by millions of people.

Great.

Feel a bit bad that I couldn't join the protesters today as I'm working (another client soon)

However I've been on previous strikes and I 100% support their work.

This book isn't about climate though, or veganism or other current views.

It's about a planet. Part of our Solar System, which we are all part of.

We can't separate ourselves from it.

Or any of the other planets.

Yes, they might be million and millions of miles away from us here on Earth.

So are little cells in our bodies. Some of them we can't even see.

But like those cells don't need our *conscious* effort to survive, neither do the planets.

Our daily existence though is dependant on us not interfering with their existence.

Just recognising that we are all part of something bigger and unexplainable.

Co-existence would be a better word.

We need each other.

Live and let live and all that.

Getting back to this morning's revelation.

If I can sustain a daily meditation practice.

A modest one of 5 minutes every morning, I know that which I seek will be revealed to me.

And that's kind of exciting!

I'm a terrible sucker for books.

Anything with 'How to' in the title will make me want to buy it as I love learning something new and teaching myself. (That's because of Mercury retrograde in my chart)

So I've bought a book all about meditation.

I already have the Dalai Lama's book about Practice, so I'm reading that again while I wait for this to arrive.

I suppose I'm a bit reticent about meditation as if seems from the outside to be so self-indulgent. All that time spent with 'the self'.

And I like company, which is one of the reasons I like my job so much because I meet so many people!

With meditation I'll have to spend time with myself. And how different will that be to keeping a journal? I know it's different but it has the same effect. Awareness of our own needs surely?

Sigh.

I suppose also I'm worried that spending too much time contemplating my inner-self won't reveal anything at all other than my thoughts bouncing around...

But

I'm prepared to give it a good go and make the most of Neptune on my Sun as I can't see any other way of making the connection.

And a further worry is; how would it be possible to read about 'how' to meditate when I already know I 'just' have to sit still for a while and 'be'.

If it were that easy surely everyone and their dog would be doing it, but they don't.

There are apps you can have on your phone, classes you can go to, groups you can join but they'll all say the same thing:

Sit

Breathe

There's not much else on the doing front that can be done.

Maybe some internal chanting or counting or visualisation or whatever.

I know the basics.

But I've never allowed myself to? Wanted to? Cared about? The subject enough to go anywhere with it.

And how can one person who meditates instruct another person?

What could they say or do to make it easier or better?

And then my mind fills with images of young girlies in leotards lying on yoga mats or doing complicated poses while looking slim, sexy and accomplished...and false.

I saw a woman this morning.

A neighbour of mine I've never seen before, returning to her home with a rolled Yoga mat in her hand and Yoga-looking clothes on and I made a mental judgement along the lines of:

"who is she kidding she's enlightened or Yogic, when she's got more money than most and time on her hands".

She was entering a house that is worth a fair bit.

And I live in an area that is now far more valuable than when we moved here.

Houses exchange hands for just above the 1/2 £million mark and rising.

And that feels wrong that our home and others are now unaffordable to 'normal' working people.

Sigh

Maybe I worry too much. Maybe my little routine will help with that

Chapter Three

Mini-Meditation Continues.
Giving-Up.
Then Acceptance

7th October 10.33am

Managed to meditate for 5 minutes every morning for more than two weeks now. Seems to fit with Neptune's energies, especially with him still going retrograde.

Time to just 'be'.

Had a week's holiday. That was nice. Found the house our father and his family lived in when he was little. I was round the back of the house taking photos when the owner came out and (quite rightly) challenged me. I introduced myself and explained what I was doing and we had a nice chat.

Today it's raining.

It's a bit strange writing a book when there is so much political turmoil in the U.K at the moment. Hubbie doesn't even want to talk about it anymore. It gets crazier everyday.

Also in the news, is climate change and how it's an emergency. Which it certainly is.

While we were away, one morning we went to the beach with our doglet. The sea had been as far up the beach as it could be and was just returning out again. Along the shoreline I saw with my own eyes something I haven't ever seen before and I felt so, so sad.

In the debris, which in the past was the occasional plastic bottle or a piece of rope, was now lots and lots of teeny, and not so teeny pieces of plastic. All colours. Mostly white. A bit of yellow here and there and some red. If I hadn't looked too closely it might have looked a bit like little pieces of shell or sand. But this wasn't shell or sand.

It was millions upon millions of teeny pieces of plastic that had obviously been in the Atlantic Ocean for so long they had got smaller and smaller, like sand does.

A shoreline of plastic pieces.

What have we done?

Plastic never, ever, ever degrades.

And this lovely shoreline was now contaminated with plastic.

Birds can eat that.

Sea creatures also won't know the difference between plastic and sea vegetables.

I recorded it on my phone and uploaded it to Twitter.

That was a very sad moment.

And it won't end it will only get worse.

In a desperate frame of mind I came home vowing not to buy things in plastic anymore.

Day Nineteen

15th October 09.59am

I'm not sure if I'm imagining things, or if the message is finally getting through, but in the last few weeks there appears to be far more interest in, and sympathy and action for the planet and the sea.

Maybe I only see on-line what I want to see but friends are posting about projects to remove plastic from the ocean. Yesterday someone I know said she was working with a new project locally to remove plastic from the coastline. Those same pieces of plastic I was writing about on the 7th.

She'd seen my post and my teenie video about North Cornwall and then told me about the project she's involved in. One chap and his girlfriend have made little sieves to sort the sand on the beach.

And a while ago I read about a little lad in the U.S.A. who had made a sea-craft to go to the plastic island in the Ocean between Hawaii and the USA and bring that plastic back to land and deal with it.

What touched me more than anything, was that these were 'normal' members of the public, with no axe to grind, who cared so much they came up with ideas and **put them into practice.**

The big trouble with the influence of Neptune as it's now retrograde is a sense of futility.

A sort of 'what's the point'....'there's nothing I can do'.... feeling.

And there's a sadness, a deep sadness to even think that we're destroying the one planet that we have.

Not intentionally.

I'm sure people aren't purposefully doing this. Anymore than someone eating burgers and chips everyday would worry about getting fat or having a heart attack.

But now seems to be the time in history when people are waking up to the nightmare that we've created.

And Neptune, in my opinion, is helping that process.

There HAS to be sadness before there can be action.

People DO have to feel the loss or the potential of loss before they're galvanised into action.

Greta Thunberg is in the USA right now.

Extinction Rebellion have been on the T.V (in a negative-reporting-mode though)

People ARE doing something.

And in my opinion it won't be the governments that do anything constructive. They'll only do something when they see all fuss that's being made 'on the ground'.

Maybe Neptune is allowing people (finally) to feel compassion?

Tuesday 22nd October 9.58am

I wouldn't say that the meditation is 'working' in that I don't feel that different. It has given me a teeny insight into my emotions and has helped me process them better.

Neptune is now one degree away from my Sun, and its retrograde. It gets to 15 degrees, the degree of my Sun on the 13th November. (*Makes a mental note to write on that day*)

With an orb of 8 degrees I'm going to be 'under' the influence for all of this year and next year and possibly until 2025. Don't really fancy spending the next 6 years writing one book, so I'd better find out more about its influence right here, right now.

As yet it hasn't hit my Mercury, so Lord knows what will happen then.

Mercury is in its detriment in Pisces, and mine is retrograde, with Neptune conjuncting that, unless I'm 100% using my intuition, things will get messy.

They might get messy anyway, so maybe meditation will allow me to access those parts of myself, and the collective unconscious that need to be expressed.

Started reading *The Power of Now* again, as Eckhart does know more about these things than I ever will and I need constant reminders of what it means to be-here-now.

And it is true all suffering disappears when in-the-now.

How can it not?

I also signed up for an online course with Future Learn about Buddhism. But I got a little frustrated with the expressions spelt in capitals such as 'The Middle Way'.

And 'The Truth'.

One lady on the course, quite rightly, asked what the 'Truth' was and no-one could give her an answer.

When you're talking about such esoteric stuff, words don't work.

You can't explain to someone what enlightenment feels like or how someone else can achieve it.

Eckhart tries really hard in his book and has made it as easy as possible, but from the other side, it's really difficult to understand it...as he says, by using your mind.

Because the mind is the thing that caused all the problems to start with.

And on paper it looks really easy:

*Stop thinking dreadful thoughts about your present situation, then you'll feel better and when you feel better things will **be** better.*

But that just doesn't work for someone who is in a crisis.., which a lot of spiritual seekers are.

They're confused and afraid and a whole host of other emotions are fuelling their search for 'Truth' and 'Meaning'.

I know because I work with lots of clients in that space and I have been there myself, numerous times.

You cannot solve a mind problem using the mind.

How crazy is that??!!

But I know it's true.

You have to use your body and forget your thoughts and release yourself into whatever flow you're in.

I understand that too.

I also understand that fighting with reality and wishing things were different, or not happening, or that they're unfair or wrong won't make things better.

That's Byron Katie's Work.

I understand all of those things too. And I can practice some of what I've learned but like other spiritual seekers I've sort of given up in a way, of finding it easy, or neat or doable 24/7

And I long for what they have.

There.

I've said it.

I wish I could 'be' enlightened.

I wonder what it actually *feels* like?

Do enlightened beings get cross that everyone else *isn't* enlightened?

Or do they have a desperate urge to tell-everyone-who-will-listen how to *also* be enlightened?

And are their lives made any better by this enlightenment?

All of these questions are mine.

And I almost have reached the part where now, after focusing on it for so long and not having any demonstrable evidence or experience I've sort of given up.

So

I give up 'trying' to be enlightened.

Did you hear that?

I'm here, right here, right now, writing this document 6 mins before my next client and without any more time to devote to it now.

I'm signing off for today.

Saturday 2nd November 15.00

I had a bit of a realisation this morning. Maybe I am *already* enlightened! Maybe the things that I know, mean I'm not struggling too much with my life at the moment.

In less than a week's time, Neptune will be exactly conjunct to my Sun sign and already it feels as if something is finally filtering through.

I haven't 'got God' or anything daft but I do feel as if the key point is not about what *happens* to me, but *who* I am.

Lots of things can happen to me and have happened but I'm still the same person, breathing the same breaths.

I wrote my Newsletter last night and tweaked it this morning. Sometimes I need to read what I write and own it.

It's all about acceptance.

Not that anyone's life miraculously changes when they accept things but in the acceptance comes a bit more peace and a little less angst.

Obviously I'm still going to feel cross if the dog rolls in some poo, or something smelly. That's a given, but I'm not going to spend my whole day fretting about it.

And I don't think acceptance stops thought.

That takes practice.

Lots.

Accepting how things are *is* enlightenment.

Arguing with reality *is* suffering.

The question is, now that I've had a teeny ah ha moment, will anything radically change?

Does it have to?

What now?

4th November 2019 12.31pm

I do feel as if I'm more 'there' than I was when I started this.

Maybe it's only by asking questions that we find answers.

Whether they are the 'correct' answers, who knows?

My Practice is now full of Taureans suffering from Uranus in their sign. It seems to have over-taken Neptune in Pisces as an urgent need.

However, Neptune is still working its theme through people's subconscious. Politicians are endlessly lying left right and centre and, probably for the first time I've ever known about, they're being challenged about their lying.

The U.K is now having a General Election. More reason to be watchful of all the promises as Mercury is now retrograde for three weeks leading up to this.

We are in such a strange place politically. Makes me feel helpless and unsafe.

I can only focus on Astrology and the 'effect' of Neptune.

Some people seem to be acutely tuned-into it, others its as if it doesn't exist.

Desperate dream this morning about our doglet being chased by a scythe-wielding nasty dog owner. I got angry and hit the owner so hard I knocked him out and then threw him over a wall. He didn't fight back. I attacked some other people too. Same result.

Then I called for our doglet and she ran back to me and I embraced her in gratitude that she was safe.

My major worry had been that her life was in danger. I woke up after holding her. Not worrying about who in the crowd of people would see me. She was my main concern.

Meditation is still happening. Made it easy for me to do and has been done faithfully for weeks now.

I'm still expecting bells and whistles but I know that isn't going to happen.

Neptune is not all about noise or fanfare. That's my Leo Ascendant talking so I've explained to it to stop searching for that.

Merging.

Aligning.

Being.

Those are things Neptune is teaching.

Am I learning that?

7th November 15.20pm

Got a few minutes before next client to write. Mercury retrograde has taken over from Neptune at the moment, even though the Moon is in Pisces, near to Neptune.

Confusion is already setting in.

Our dog food delivery company sent me last month's invoice, again.

My app provider has randomly started charging me VAT for the service they provide...and they're not even based in the UK and as I did my tax return I found other anomalies, where they gain from 'rounding' up and I lose out.

However the Sun is out which always cheers things up a little.

According to Eckhart Tolle I don't need to 'do' anything to be enlightened, I already am and so are lots of other people that have stopped believing their thoughts.

It does take some practice to do that.

Not believe thoughts...when I think about where they came from, and they might not have actually originated in my own mind, but someone else's, it does make it easier to question.

Do I know what 'peaceful' feels like?

Is that a Neptune word?

War certainly isn't Neptunian.

That's Mars territory.

8th November 2019 13.58

It's a lovely sunny day today. Autumn sunshine always makes a difference to people's moods, mine included.

It means I can see things around the house without needing to turn a light on.

Neptune is still retrograding and on the 27th it will be 15 degrees and as near to my Sun, again, as it can before it goes direct on the 28th.

My Sun, as already mentioned is 15 degrees and 6 minutes into Pisces so already Neptune at 16 degrees today, is conjunct my Sun.

I don't know if it will feel any different when it starts going direct again.

But today, all-feels-well.

It might be because I've got some household tasks done, I've recorded some audio for my Audio Book and as I said the Sun is definitely shining...

Bless

Who is expressing Neptune the most clearly now I wonder?

Neptune is nicely transiting Greta Thunberg's Sun 12 degrees and Moon 16 degrees of Capricorn and forming a sextile aspect.

Is that helping?

Is it her?

I can't think of anyone in the 'public eye' in the UK who is.

Politicians are falling over themselves to make the most convincing noises. All that will change as we get into December and I expect things will, again, become vicious and combative.

9th November 11.34am

It's raining, a rather Neptune in Pisces-retrograde thing. I forgot to mention yesterday that we've had flooding in the UK, which would be a Neptune thing.

Neptune rules anything to do with water.

He is after all the Water God.

It seems fitting that this is happening now.

Yesterday I was wondering who might be 'speaking' the truth of Neptune and as far as I see it, the current weather conditions are. The people involved in the aftermath: residents and emergency workers having to 'deal' with its effects.

Storm Desmond broke a new record for national rainfall accumulation on 5th December 2015 for a dropping as much as 34cm of rain in 24 hours in Cumbria. This continued into early 2016 7.

Neptune had already been in Pisces for 4 years.

We've now had more floods in the last ten years than ever in the U.K and as usual no politician seems to be taking any of it seriously.

Obviously no-one can stop the rain but the UK is criss-crossed with numerous rivers that now just can't cope when extreme rain lands onto the ground and filters into them.

We don't live anywhere near any rivers because we live up a hill...but there's nothing to stop extreme rainfall from flooding our house as it could easily roll off the road outside, into our property.

And it's younger people that are the most affected, as they might not have house-contents insurance or even understand how to protect themselves from extreme weather.

I know so few young people that even own wellies !

We see it every year at Glastonbury with the Homoeopathic Charity I volunteer with.

Certain city-based younger people aged 19-30, turn up carrying vast quantities of 'stuff' not realising that they have to walk with their belongings across miles of fields to reach their camping site.

And if it rains, which it can, the whole site turns into a mud-bath.

And they don't know how to cope.

It'll seem 'fun' for 12 hours until they're totally soaked through, their clothes have no-where to dry, they get cold and their feet are wet.

We worked with one lad who had trench foot. He was working as a volunteer rubbish-collector and he didn't have wellies.

His feet were so wet they'd started to rot.

Piles of skin were peeling away from his feet and they hurt.

We treated him the best we could but the only solution would have been to go home, get dry and seek medical help ASAP.

23rd November 2019 2.44pm

The U.K. is falling into more and more lies and dis-information. People don't even appear surprised about it anymore.

An election is on its way next month and politicians are parading on the television, spouting whatever comes into their heads.

It's mightily depressing.

I've been making an audio-book and doing my best to make it fulfil the audio requirements for publication.

In comparison, writing books is as easy as pie.

In re-reading for the umpteen time *The Power of Now*

I've now come to the conclusion I don't need to 'do' anything to sense Neptune better, or even reach enlightenment.

I'm already there, so I can stop searching.

There is nothing more I need to 'do' other than to recognise that enlightenment isn't some weird type of attainment, it's a form of acceptance.

That I am a human being, with a body and my soul is something completely different.

My soul is your soul is everyone else's soul because there is no separation, there is no 'me' and 'you'...we are all one.

Sounds a bit corny writing it like that...

We are all stardust.

That seems more hopeful, more uplifting.

And I really want to feel more uplifted and only I can create that, for me, in my world.

The other thing that has occurred to me is everyone has a different experience of their spiritual path.

Their belief.

There are similarities, but they're as varied as humans themselves.

Luckily animals don't beat themselves up in the same way we do about this.

Chapter Four

New Year & The End-of-The-World Dream

Saturday

11-01-2020 4pm

I'm a bit cross with myself now because I haven't written for 2 months. Xmas got in the way, then New Year and I also recorded an audio version of one of my books.

I got very dispirited about the General Election, which is now all over and we have to bear another 5 years of Tory control... and Trump has decided to get the USA involved with Iran.... again.

Putting all of this aside, I am now nearly in my 60th year of existence. The clock is ticking but Neptune doesn't appear to be at all bothered about this.

I've also closed my Homeopathy practice and am now concentrating on Astrology and Hypnotherapy and I love the fact that I'm also teaching Astrology one-on-one.

Long may that continue!

I feel O.K in myself...apart from *not* writing this.

The planets this year are also totally different to last year and with the year starting with five of them in the sign of Capricorn, they're all making a nice sextile to Neptune.

And Uranus, even though it's such a disruptive planet, is also forming a nice sextile to Neptune, so that feels rather comfortable in a strange sort of way.

Another plus point is I've let go of all of the clients I was struggling to help and have referred them on.

I now only work with people that I like or can easily help.

I do feel that in my later years I don't have the patience to help people that won't, can't or don't help themselves...

Also Neptune is working its way towards my Mercury...

How will things be then?

Will I start having (even more) weird dreams?

Will I get more inspired?

I do know that too much Neptune can make people lose touch with reality and I don't fancy that as an outcome.

I'm nearly also at the end of my second Saturn Return.

I've make arrangements with my financial advisor and put my affairs in order.

In a few weeks time I would have been retired and entitled to the state pension.

When I first started work, women retired at 60.

Not anymore.

Someone in government pushed for it to be raised to 66, so that's too far away now to even think about.

There have been fires in Australia and floods in the U.K. and the climate emergency doesn't seem to have any impact on governments. Everyone is still carrying on, talking about some future date when things will be sorted.

Stupid dates too.

'We will be CO2 efficient in 2030'.

That's 10 years away!

We could all be living on boats by then!

It really doesn't take long for homes to be destroyed with bad weather conditions...

I can barely think about or read about it anymore, as it's so distressing especially when wildlife is also destroyed, never to be replaced.

Sigh.

Friday

17-01-2020 1.53pm

Oh Lord, I'm speedily zooming into a complete depression.

Yesterday I dreamt the world had ended. Or to be exact, was just about to end.

I dreamt I was outside looking up at the sky, which was grey and full of smoke and dark clouds.

I was with a younger woman who was urging me to look at the blue sky to the right but the sky ahead and above was grey and smoky.

I didn't want to look at the blue sky because I knew the world was ending and the sky was the sign.

I shouted: "I don't want the world to end"...and I woke up.

And the forests are burning in Australia and the Amazon.

And the skies have been grey and full of rain where we live and it's unnaturally warm for January and nothing feels right.

Is this Neptune?

How can that be inspirational and awe-inspiring?

It feels desolate and depressing.

I also feel as if everything I've created is second-class and scrappy.

A few weeks ago I felt as if I'd got everything in-the-bag and I knew where I was and what I was doing and how I was feeling.

Now it feels as if all that is slipping away.

I feel old and useless.

I also feel as if I've lost part of my identity by not being a Homeopath anymore as I stopped that on the 31st December 2019

And I don't feel as if I have a 'message' anymore either and that any message I might have is worthless.

What self-indulgent thinking this is!!

Where is the wave going?

There is always a wave with Neptune. It creates a wave of inspiration and creativity.

Steiner managed to use its energy constructively.

And I've tried so many times to read a Steiner book and understand it. And it's hard.

Some of the things he says don't seem to make sense.

Am I not making sense?

How confused am I?

I don't *think* I feel confused.

I feel rudderless.

As if I've rowed out into the middle of an enormous lake and I've accidently dropped my oar into the deep, deep water and my boat is stuck, in the centre of this cold, gloomy, expansive lake. And if I want to make it back to the shore, I'm going to have to paddle with my hands. Which will take me ages and wear me out. I certainly can't swim. It's too deep and cold and I can't swim far anyway. There's no immediate danger. No winds or bad weather. But the Sun has disappeared and it's just me, the boat, and the quiet, deadly-quiet lake.

If I had access to magic I suppose I'd magic up either a gentle breeze to blow me back to the shore or some kind porpoise or dolphin (except they don't live in lakes) or maybe a beaver? That would push my boat to the edge of the lake.

But I feel as if I've lost my access to magic.

It all feels pointless.

Thursday

30th Jan 2020

I feel as if I've dropped down a rabbit hole into an alternative universe.

Someone I know reasonably well turned up at ours over the weekend, splosed out of their brain and collapsed onto my office chair.

Two policemen visited after someone in their family rang them.

That was bad enough.

The older policeman said they couldn't remove the person from our house as they weren't actually committing a crime and we'd just have to wait until they woke up.

The policemen left.

So when the person didn't respond to their name or shaking and with their breathing being imperceptible, I rang for an ambulance. They were so unresponsive even the first responder who quickly arrived couldn't get any replies.

Eventually they were taken to hospital but apparently this has been repeatedly happening over the last few weeks.

I went round a few times afterwards for welfare checks, then another member of the family became suicidal...

Worried about them repeatedly collapsing all over the place. Alcohol is the reason and is being used as a solution to their problems but is obviously only making them worse.

I want to take them to the local drugs and alcohol clinic that I volunteered at but that's my wish, not there's.

So it's just usual platitudes and typical English politeness that is preventing me from sweeping them up, in the car and driving them over there and getting them get the help they need.

But of course, if they don't want help, who am I to offer it?

Spent 4-5 days in a dilemma.

How far is too far?

Emails have gone adrift, as my domain name has an issue. I moved from one host to another and now my domain name isn't working and I can't find the solution.... yet.

I went to pay for some tea in a cafe this morning with my debit card and the transaction got refused...assistant tried again and it went through O.K.

Neptune *and* Venus are now on my Sun sign and all the planets are today on the right-hand side of my chart.

I feel a little frazzled.

It's a weird feeling. As if I'm between the devil and the deep blue sea.

More sea than devil but it's as if I'm languishing in that lake again.

I also feel as if I'm repeating myself. This feeling comes on when my B12 jab is due, which it isn't.

Are these my feelings or the problem person?

Where do they start and where do I end?

I also don't seem able to focus on anything for more than a few moments without getting easily distracted.

Tomorrow is the last day that we're part of the European Union.

Adrift, on our own, with no European neighbours.

And so much confusion.

Phone professional insurers and talked about the name-change of my business and what to do...then when I got back this morning someone else from their office left a message about the self-same issue.

Had to ring again and clearly state what was needed and that person who'd phoned didn't need to ring and was my insurance OK?

None of this is desperately important. It's not life or death for goodness sake.

Adrift.

Alone.

Wanting deep sleep and fun dreams.

I can *feel* Neptune now and it's a very strange feeling.

I'd happily go to sleep now but it's lunchtime and I need to eat, not sleep.

Maybe I need to send myself some Reiki or call upon the Unseen Therapist to help.

Maybe that's what I need to do.

Light a candle for myself, not troubled people or clients.

Or maybe, in *addition* to troubled people and clients.

Pisces.

I'm a reformed Pisces, not an out-of-control one.

Lunch.

Put away the washing.

Tidy up.

Get practical

Problems don't get solved by thinking about them.

Be grateful.

I AM grateful.

Peace.

Just had a text from troubled person to say their suicidal sibling is coming over later today to be with them.

Seems fitting.

Healer friend has also lit three candles for them and sent love and care *"Tell them I pray for their quick recovery, and hug them for me please."*

There are lovely people in the world and I need to focus on that and them:)

Extra Peace.

Now I feel tearful as troubled person replied to text and said "Oh Bless her, Mary".

Glad they feel good for that sweet gesture.

There does need to be more sweetness in my world and that's a lovely example.

I am blessed.

Wednesday

5th Feb 2020 12.44pm

Troubled person has politely refused help, which didn't surprise me. Made me wonder if I'd been *too* helpful.

With Neptune right on my Sun sign, I was wondering if their dilemma? Experience? Is somehow a great version of projection of how this planet can affect me?

The negative side of Neptune certainly is to slip, slide or dive into overwhelming emotions and resort to the oblivion that alcohol brings.

Why would my help be accepted anyway?

What makes my suggestion any better than anything else in their life that they've experienced?

My Leo Ascendant is certainly struggling with it, so I've had to remind myself constantly that none of this is my fault and there is nothing that I can do to make *them* better so maybe making *myself* feel better would be a smarter decision.

I suppose if they hadn't collapsed onto my office chair and the police hadn't been called by another family member and if the paramedic hadn't arrived and the ambulance... I'd have found it easier to let this go...

I feel a sort of sadness because I know what it feels like to feel bad and helpless and at a loss.

And now when I know it's possible to recover from those feelings and someone isn't biting my hand off to also feel that relief, I feel a failure.

Sigh

I'll have to take this to supervision and the worst thing is, this isn't even a patient of mine!

Extra sigh.

I suppose I feel helpless...

I hadn't forced anything.

And they certainly *can* refuse help...

Why am I beating myself up?

I'm not suffering so why am I worrying about someone else's suffering?

Maybe they're not suffering.

And even if they are suffering, why do I think I can relieve that suffering?

Space.

I need to give this and me some space.

Crowding myself in isn't going to work.

I probably also need to get out of the house for a while.

I always feel better sorting a problem out in a different location.

Chapter Five

Pandemic & More Confusion

Monday

23-3-2020 16.29

Oh my goodness I don't know where to start...

The corona virus has now spread ALL over the world. COVID-19 it's called. I'm using words and phrases I didn't even know the meaning of a month ago

This is Neptune ramping up its message...

Self-isolating

Pandemic

Toilet-roll panic-buying

Checked the planets and found out that it's to do with Uranus in Taurus.

All the other Astrologers are writing about planets in Capricorn: Pluto, Jupiter, Mars and Saturn but today Saturn reached Aquarius...it'll go retrograde in a couple of months.

BUT the Capricorn planets are NOT the cause of this virus' ability to spread so quickly and so deeply.

It's a joint effort between Uranus=freedom and Neptune=psychic connection.

Everyone is feeling connected. Maybe not in a positive way.

Maybe only via panic but they're copying each other and ordering online and going bonkers in shops.

Europe is infected.

Italy has 5,476 deaths and infections at 60,000

Spain has 1,720 deaths and 28,572

And those figures are increasing by the day.

I don't want to mention the numbers. I want to talk about the planets and the people.

First I had an accident on my motorbike. Taxi crossed the road into my path and I swerved to miss it and hit the curb.

Driver zoomed off. Didn't stop. Probably didn't even know I'd narrowly missed him and had fallen off.

Then the front door lock jammed on Saturday morning.

Engineer came today and couldn't fix it.

Saturday evening we had a power cut and this Wednesday our water will be turned off for 24 hours.

Previous Homeopathy clients have got back in touch.

One from 13 years ago!

I've got the message Universe!

I'm back at work online taking cases and sending out remedies for sore throats coughs, sleeplessness, anxiety and skin complaints.

The Astrology practice certainly hasn't slowed down.

One part of me so wants to help the suffering.

The other part of me is obsessively reading everything I can about the virus and where it's spreading.

We are 'self-isolating' now.

Got no choice because the door is jammed locked shut anyway.

My sister has it.

My nephew, his wife and baby also have it and one of my student's husband.

Fear.

I don't know how scary Neptune actually is but I suppose the combination of that and Uranus is accelerating something.

Thursday
26-3-2020 11.46am
We are locked-in.
Literally.
Door engineer couldn't fix the problem...has gone off and left us with a non-functioning front door.
He's removed the key barrel.

All businesses are closed.

Everyone has to stay at home, but not that many people seem to be managing it that well.

Everyone seems to be treating it like they're imprisoned.

Which is strange really...

Some people seem to be taking to the idea of 'home-imprisonment' like a duck to water.

Others are getting into dreadful panics.

Set aside some time this Friday to do a Facebook Live session talking about how to stay at home without going bonkers, by using the 4th house of home as an indicator.

Finding it hard to concentrate long enough to write these entries.

Doing my best not to feel overwhelmed.

Swinging between being fine, then reading far too many scary stories online then swinging to anxiety and wanting-to-help-everyone.

When I'm well aware, if I think clearly, that the only person who I need to help, is myself.

And if I look after myself well, then I won't need to worry about anyone else.

Touché

Writing this now, when the sun is shining outside is a bit hard.

Maybe I need to top-up my B12 levels.

That generally stops me being so anxious.

Had a nice dog walk this morning with my bestie. Have an audio-book to finish.

Editing to do for an article.

Charts to get ready for a student session and a new client for next week.

I'm not short of things to 'do' but I'm terribly short of concentration.

I'm flitting from one thing to another. My Gemini Moon isn't enjoying the fact that everyday could be the same as every other day.

Wake up

Wash

Eat breakfast.

Dog walk.

Tea and snack

Write (which is what I'm actually doing now)

Have more tea.

Read articles online, post on social media, text friends and family.

Have lunch

More reading while eating lunch.

More worrying....

Make dinner.

Relax with doggie on spare bed and crochet while listening to audio-books/podcasts.

I see where I'm making a big mistake

Too much time on my phone reading stuff that

a) won't make me feel better

b) will snatch and steal good writing time away from me, when a lock-down is the IDEAL time to engage with this process properly.

Sunday

29-3-2020 10.24am

Now I totally realise not only why I started to write this account *before* the virus hit as there I was asking for the Universe to 'give me a sign'...remember how I started wanting to 'be' enlightened and wondering what enlightenment is all about...when BANG it happened and this virus is teaching me so much.

Went for a walk, as always, this morning.

I always do the morning walkies with our Saluki X Whippet rescue dog.

Today we all went together.

Hubbie, me and the dog.

Hubbie kept saying how lovely it was and how quiet and how there wasn't any traffic fumes and how nice it was to be there outdoors and *not* meet (many) other human beings.

He has Sun in the 8th and would be perfectly happy in an uninhabited Universe with just me, him and our doglet.

I, however, was missing meeting up with other dog walkers and having a bit of a chat.

(Moon in Gemini, Sun in the 7th)

We did come across a neighbour standing outside the local mini-supermarket.

He was waiting for his wife. We had a little chat and carried on walking home. The only other people we saw were joggers and dog walkers.

I know it's Sunday.

I also know we left the house rather early and the clocks went back last night BUT there's normally a few cars here and there.

Not today.

Zero.

It certainly looks like a shot from an apocalypse film.

And the fear is palpable when you meet other people.

Two metres apart.

"Don't come near me I may catch the dreaded virus".

However, what this virus and Neptune is bringing home to me very forcefully is that we are all connected.

Very connected.

We might live in our own little bubbles but Neptune-in-Pisces is shining a light on the simple fact that we DO all need each other.

That we ARE all connected.

And if one link in the chain connecting us breaks, then the whole of civilization is thrown into chaos.

Having looked at various other epidemics I can safely say that Neptune in the planet that represents some of them.

The cholera epidemic hit the UK in 1848 when Neptune entered Pisces.

In the flu epidemic of 1918, Neptune was in the sign of Pisces conjunct Saturn.

The third outbreak of the plague Neptune was conjunct Pluto.

In all of these outbreaks the thing that keeps coming back into view is the Importance of Clean Water.

In the UK in this present pandemic all the government videos and statements are urging people to wash their hands.

Such a simple thing to do.

But I know from my own private practice that not many people actually do it properly.

I've had clients come to my home-office and make a quick visit to the loo and I can *hear* that they haven't activated the taps.

I'm sure if I'd asked them, they would have said they had but I can hear the taps turn on from my office and I know they haven't done it!

Plus UK residents are rubbish at hand-washing.

Only last week the PM was espousing on live TV how to wash hands, then exactly one week later, he comes down with the present virus.

There has even been research on hand-washing which proves people do not wash their hands after going to the loo. 8.

The World Health Organisation had stressed even in 2012 that hand washing prevents epidemics more readily than any other activity 9

But still people ignore this sage advice.

And maybe that's what Neptune just wants us to know.

How important water is.

As it helps us stay clean and hydrated.

In fact how valuable water sources are.

Which then leads into the consideration that safe water is becoming more and more scarce.

Sigh.

I've finished an online course with Future Learn about COVID and one quote struck me as important:

He's using 'water' language:

"And as the risk spreads to other countries who are now going through the beginnings of the first wave, then you will find actually different of these ripples travelling in different directions."

Prof Gabriel Leung, Dean of the Li Ka Shing Faculty of Medicine of the University of Hong Kong

Tuesday

31-3-2020, 9.40pm

I've now got a headache. Was working online today and also did choir practice online and now I'm severely sick of looking at a screen.

Turned the brightness down on my monitor in the hope that this will help.

Covid-19 is spreading and it seems as if our government has run out of ideas of what to do to help.

It's almost as if our PM has run out of steam about it all and is bored. Trump seems to be doing the same thing (they're both Gemini's)

I'm convinced that Neptune is part of this COVID-19 thing and I'm in the process of writing an article about it.

This book started out with me wanting to understand Neptune and now a few months later Neptune is speaking REALLY clearly and absolutely no-one is listening.

Am I the only one to hear the message?

That we are ALL connected?

It doesn't matter where in the world we're located.

We're all part of the same human race.

I'm also now beginning to get a bit stir crazy. I don't know where that expression came from but I know it's used to describe how you feel when you've been indoors for too long...

Sigh

Tuesday

7th April 2020 11.57am

The Prime Minister has been rushed to hospital into intensive care as his COVID-19 symptoms worsened. Last night he had 4 litres of oxygen. He's not on an incubator.... yet.

The country is lurching from one crisis to another.

No-one seems to be planning for this rationally or helpfully.

Only the Queen seemed to have any sense of what's needed now.

Neptune will go retrograde in June. Then what?

We are still stuck in the house. No real problem. Compared to actually having the virus I think I'd choose self-isolation over virus any day.

Then Uranus will go retrograde in August.

This isn't going to just disappear overnight.

It's a lovely sunny day today.

Took the doggie for a walk with a friend (keeping our 2 metre distance) over the fields this morning. Half of the local dog population obviously had the same idea.

My practice is as busy as ever and podcast listeners are booking sessions and lessons.

I'm glad I trained in more than one discipline as it means depending on the climate, I can help in whatever way is needed.

Practising Horary Astrology now.

Might need some clients to practice on!

Overwhelm is the biggest side-effect of Neptune and there are times I feel a little that way, but then I remember to slow down, only do that's necessary, turn off my phone, stop reading the news.... and breathe...

Week Three of lock-down but a big chunk of the country isn't taking it seriously.

It's hard though to take Neptune's energies seriously.

It's not going to knock any sense into people.

In fact it might have totally the opposite effect.

Make them dreamy and impractical.

I've run out of sugar-free squash.

Seems so weird not to be able to zoom into town on my bike and go to Waitrose and buy another bottle.

Buying things I use now has become a sort of competitive sport.

Will it stock it?

Will they post it?

Will it arrive before I run out of XYZ?

Literally missing seeing other people's faces face-to-face.

Monday

20th April 12.24pm

Is it a month we've been locked-down, locked-in now?

Seems much longer than that.

Almost can't remember what it feels like to *not* social distance or answer the door or just jump in the car for a drive.

Sun is now in Taurus.

Neptune is still chugging through Pisces. That will go on for a long, long time so I better get used to it.

Read something very meaningful about being-in-the-moment.

Because actually that's the only place we can actually be.

Anywhere else that our minds go to, isn't right here right now.

I was reading a post by Thich Nhat Hanh and he was talking/ writing about enlightenment.

He said

"Enlightenment is available in every moment. There is no way to enlightenment. Enlightenment is the way.

Enlightenment is not far away.

It can be immediate with mindfulness.

Breathing in you can have enlightenment. No thinking. No planning. No fear. Then your concentration becomes stronger." 10

So, it isn't something that I need to 'do' or to 'think'. It's just being where I am now, at my computer, writing this to you (and myself) now. Breathing in as I do it. Breathing out...

Looking out of the window and seeing the Sun shining on the road and the front garden.

That's all there is to it?

Just being here?

Right here right now?

So, why doesn't the world open up before me and lines of singing angels rise above my head?

Why don't I feel like I felt when I was in my 20s and everything made sense?

Where has that feeling gone?

Why do I *so* want to feel it now?

I do my 5 mins meditation every morning.

I read all the books and articles.

I'm constantly searching for this 'thing' that doesn't want to be found.

Maybe because it just isn't as hidden as I thought it was.

Maybe it *is* here, right here, right now.

In this moment.

This beautiful moment of writing to you, whoever you are and sharing my experience with you.

Maybe I need to realise that beauty, because if I'm dead I won't feel it. It's part of being alive. And I'm definitely alive at the moment.

Sunday

10th May 2020 1.21.pm

The PM is going to make an announcement today about the lock-down. Something about garden centres opening and libraries. All my library-worker friends aren't happy about that.

I'm part of a campaign group to keep libraries open with proper funding and staffing and last year and the year before we spent lots of time keeping Bath Central Library from closing. Now all of a sudden, during a pandemic, country leaders are realising how important they are...but once again are ignoring the actual people that work in them.

On the plus side, there are planets in Air signs: Venus in Gemini and Mars in Aquarius. Venus will be there for a number of months, so that's a happy time for me as I have Moon in Gemini.

I seem to have got past wanting enlightenment. As if that wish has now passed me by now that something far more important has happened:

A curtailing to my personal freedom.

I'm more than well aware of how important social distancing is and how we do need to, maybe for years yet, avoid close contact with people we are not related to or living with.

Of course that are idiots who are so entrenched with their ideas of freedom that they're meeting up and protesting about their freedom being removed.

But really.

Has it?

Freedom to get in the car?

Freedom to have a party?

Freedom to get on an aeroplane and travel here and there?

Is that really what's at stake and are those things really THAT important?

I don't think so.

Surely keeping people from catching the virus is a number one priority or is it all about YOU and no-one else?

Surely this is a collective experience? That we are all experiencing? And it's not the same as imprisonment or incarceration.

I'm not going to protest about that.

If me staying at home stops my family and friends from dying, then that's a 'sacrifice' I'm perfectly happy to make!

In August Uranus goes retrograde and I expect if things have returned to 'normal' by then, there will be another wave of this virus.

On June 23rd Neptune goes retrograde until the end of November so either or both of these dates will be significant as far as the virus goes.

Thursday

14th May 2020 10.23am

Nice country walk then tea in the garden. Seems a bit criminal to be living like this when so many people are living with the uncertainty and loss that this virus has brought.

Neptune is now 20 degrees 32 into Pisces and my Sun sign is 15 degrees and my Mercury is 24 so Neptune is right slap bang between these two planets of mine.

How does that make me feel?

Well I'm not too sure.

What I do know is strange things are happening. A friend of mine, who we are in a book club together with, suggested that the next book we read should be *Thinking Fast & Slow* by Daniel Kahneman. I looked at the cover when she sent me the details and thought *'I recognise that cover, I'm sure I've read that book'.*

I agreed to read it as I don't have a copy anymore and is the sort of non-fiction book I like reading in our book group.

A few days later or even maybe it was the next day, losing track of days now, an author emailed me and said they'd read my review on Amazon for *Thinking Fast and Slow* and would I like to read his book, which is similar?

Now what are the chances of choosing a book to read, then days later (I'll check in a min how long ago it was) someone emails me about the very book we've decided on?

It wasn't as if I'd posted on social media or written about it on my Twitter account but someone emails me about the very book we've been chatting about.

Chances?

Rather slim.

Plus the fact that the book was published in 2017 and I'd not only already read it but also reviewed it as I'd enjoyed it so much...

Then I started to realise that our thoughts aren't really our own.

We think we have them exclusively in our minds...when we don't!

They broadcast all over the ether or thought-waves-world, whatever you want to call it.

I suppose there really aren't words for this process.

My thoughts become my reality.

Literally!

And another one I had a while ago was I was a tad bored and asked the Universe for something exciting and creative to happen and our choir leader emailed about another choir who are organising a mass virtual choir.

That sounded really up my street so I immediately signed-up for that experience.

Wonderful!

I have all the equipment to do it.

The singing ability too.

I was trained as a soprano and had singing lessons when I was very young...

So a) I'm not afraid of performing and singing.

b) I know how to sing in tune.

And the song we had to learn for the virtual choir is a beautiful, simple song with a lovely message and I *really* enjoyed practicing it and preparing, recording, uploading it.

Yum.

That absolutely filled that gap for me and now our choir want to do something similar with another haunting song.

Fab.

My choir leader even sent me a lovely email complementing me on my version and said he had

"tears in my eyes... you sang with such purity and conviction that I was really moved by it."

Awww that absolutely made my year hearing/reading that! Which has spurred me on to learning the song he wants us to perform.

Just because we are locked-down doesn't mean we can't be creative and the thing that's making this all worth it for me are the people who are *being* creative during this time.

The ones letting their creativity flow and not worrying about what other people might think or is-this-the-right-way-to-do-this?

And just doing whatever it is that they want to do.

However, sadly the government are being as helpful and honest as a wet flannel, and worse they seem committed to make things as confusing and ambiguous as possible, meanwhile hundreds of people are still dying every day :(

Chapter Six

Listening to & Hearing Neptune

Saturday

6th June 2020 9.58am

Haven't managed to get anywhere near this record for days and days.

Been spending too much time following the news, which gets worse every single day.

Planning on attending a Black Lives Protest this afternoon and in true Pisces-style with Neptune in Pisces transiting Sun and Mercury I decided NOT to tell my husband because I don't want him to worry about me catching the COVID-19

Mars is now in Pisces, conjuncting my Sun and Mercury too and I do feel cross about police brutality towards black people.

And who *wouldn't* be moved in some way seeing an unarmed black man killed by a white police officer, with two other officers watching and doing *nothing*?

Just like the virus swept from country to country, the anger, frustration, despair and grief about racism has swept from the USA to the UK.

Except the virus came to U.K. shores before it went to U.S.A.

All the outer planets are happily speaking to each other.

Pluto in stoic, pragmatic earth sign Capricorn is happily communicating with Uranus in fellow practical, steady earth sign Taurus and Neptune in floppy, emotional water sign Pisces is adding empathy to the mix.

It surely is a winning combination for change?

The young people that vitalised the vegan and environmental movement are now joining forces again to protest against racism.

All of this is being helped by Saturn being in freedom-loving Aquarius.

Taking responsibility for our freedoms.

Being real about the restrictions that white privilege has smothered the voice of black people.

And now, this month six planets are going to go retrograde.

Then what?

Last time that happened was 1984, when the UK miners rebelled against Margaret Thatcher shutting the mines and there were protests and strikes.

One part of me wants to finish this book but it feels unfinished because the transit through Neptune is still happening and as a serious Astrologer, I want to record how it played out in the UK.

For me

I can only ever report about, or even write about what I know, or see, or hear or come across.

So, with my Astrologer hat on, and with the Moon being in freedom loving, international, philosophical Sagittarius today, squaring Neptune/Mars in Pisces I will be a very small witness to the Black Lives Matter protest in Bath today.

Wednesday

24th June 2020, 8.24pm

Neptune started retrograding yesterday and by the end of November it'll go all the way back to 18 degrees 5 degrees.

My Mercury is 24 degrees so it will do a little dance between the two planets for the next five months.

With six planets retrograding and Venus coming out tomorrow, as soon as one goes direct, another seems to take its place.

Plus Mercury is retrograde until July 12th.

Will I still be writing this then?

I don't seem to be able to finish this book.

Is it a book?

No clients this week.

Not even a student.

I had blocked the week off on my calendar and booking app, then changed my mind and unblocked it. Now I have an empty week so there really is no excuse not to write, which is why I'm here, rather later than normal trying to make some sense of the last few weeks.

The government want everyone to go back to work.

Which seems rash considering a few weeks ago we all had to stay home and isolate.

The virus is still there. People are still catching it and still dying.

Nothing has changed.

Maybe less people are dying, but there's still the risk...

Things are still strange and seem to filter through the Neptune influence.

People contact me that I think about.

But that happens to lots of people so it's not especially unique.

I do feel happier with myself.

Less anxious about me.

Less grumpy with my husband.

Some things just aren't worth getting bothered about.

It's very hot today. Hottest day so far this year. And it's still sunny outside even though it's early evening.

Been reading books by black authors to help me learn more about Black Lives.

I knew things were bad. Reading about their struggles makes it even more real.

I'm working completely online now.

I don't even want to see clients face-to-face now. The risk seems too great and everything I did face-to-face I can do online or by phone.

Is that Uranus in Taurus?

Using technology for practical purposes?

It'll all be fine until we run out of electricity or the Internet crashes.

It can't be eternal, nothing is.

Still having struggling dreams. Travelling to places I can't reach. Being in buildings I can't access all of. Running. Flying. Travelling in vehicles. Motion. Anxious.

Unsatisfied. Troubled.

No one really knows what's happening. Conspiracy theories abound.

Lots of talk about 'getting back to normal'.

But there won't be any normal ever again. This is how things are now for years and years.

Maybe until the end of this Neptune transit.

Until we realise that we are all connected.

That we're all part of the same planet.

All flesh and blood and tears and hopes, fears and wishes.

Who is listening to Neptune?

Everyone seems to be tuning out. Ignoring the message. Not hearing. Putting the message to one side and hoping that by ignoring it, it'll just go away.

But that's not how Neptune works.

Neptune is there to get us to transcend and we can't do that while we're too busy to listen.

I wish I could hear and be able to write what Neptune wants us to hear.

Maybe I have already.

Through the experiences and the thoughts I have had during the time I have spent on this project.

Maybe I have.

Maybe.

Chapter Seven

Astrological Enlightenment Tips

Q. Do I need to be a Pisces to experience enlightenment?

A. No. Of course you don't! Any sign of the Zodiac can question the validity of their life and strive for self-awareness, then experience other realms of existence.

Q. Astrologically, when would be the best time to start my quest?

A. Jupiter is another planet that governs spirituality, along with Neptune. You could start working on your spiritual path when Jupiter or Neptune reaches your Sun sign, Moon sign or Mercury sign, or even when they pass over your Ascendant, Descendant, MC or IC.

As these are critical points in your chart, they will be felt when Jupiter or Neptune transits over them.

Q. What should I be seeking?

A. Compassion for humanity. Forgiveness. Awareness. Peace. Tranquillity. Kindness.

Any spiritual teaching will suggest that anger, impatience, hate, annoyance and irritation are not conducive to reaching inner peace and would need to addressed and healed in some way.

Q. Is there an end point?

A. No. Enlightenment isn't somewhere or something to be reached. It's a path that you choose to walk knowing that in the searching for it, you can be guided in that direction. It's only when we ask a question that an answer will be sought and maybe found, just for today. But then, are we asking the right question? And will we be satisfied with the answer? A spiritual path is one of asking, and then acceptance. Continual questioning won't get us there quicker or faster. Maybe rephrasing the question or even reversing it will help. See Byron Katie https://thework.com/for more info on this.

Q. How long does it take?

A. Ha ha! I thought it would take 30 days of concentrated effort! 18 months later I'm still walking that path!

Q. Is it worth the effort, will I feel any better?

A. For sure. Definitely. You will feel better as you'll be observing yourself, your life, other's lives, weather, hopes wishes and dreams, death, destruction, love and compassion.

And in being aware and observing, not getting drawn into tragedies or hurts, these things in your life will feel more meaningful and eloquent.

I could say you'll feel lighter but that implies that heaviness is negative or unwanted. You might feel lighter but not in a physical way. Less inclined to sweat the small stuff. More likely to be accepting of what is, rather than fighting it. Finding ways continually to present yourself as open, alert and taking part in your life, rather than wishing-it-was-different. Acceptance isn't giving-up, it's far more powerful than that. Acceptance stops the continual fights going on in your mind. It allows movement. All things will change and this too soon will pass.

Acknowledgements

I would like to thank the following people:

For those who kindly read through the first, very rough draft of this book:

Amanda Gates, Diana Anderson, Julie Lee and Maz Brown.

Thank you for taking the time to help me and for your continued and valued support of my work.

Izzy Daly for coming up with a beautiful cover design that really spoke in Neptune's language.

My super sister Dr Lucy English BA, MA PhD for her encouraging words.

My sister Emily for all the yummy treats!

My husband Jonathan for his never-ending love.

My son S for being his wonderful Libran self.

My friends Mabel, Usha and Anna for being such good mates.

My friend Mandy, thank you for our weekly non-fiction book-reading meet-ups and for your compassion.

My friends Laura and Phil for lovely days out in the countryside.

Deep appreciation goes to Emma Foster and Dwayne Kerr for agreeing to include Neriah's Astro chart.

Thank you also to all my clients, students, subscribers and podcast listeners.

You are the reason I do what I do.

References

1. Astrology for All, Alan Leo, reprint, fourth edition, 1910 L.N. Fowler and Co

2. The Art of Synthesis, Alan Leo, reprint, 1938

3. The Modern Text Book of Astrology, Margaret E. Hone, 1951, L.N.Fowler & Co Ltd, Romford Essex, reprinted 1980, The Camelot Press Ltd, Southampton

4. Astrology The Stars and Human Life: A Modern Guide, Christopher Mc Intosh, 1970, Macdonald Unit 75, London W.1.

5. The New Waite's Compendium of Natal Astrology with Ephemeris for 1880-1980 and Universal Table of Houses, Colin Evans, revised and brought up to date by Brian E. F. Gardener, 1971, Routledge & Kegan Paul Limited, London.

6. Cosmos and Psyche, Intimations of a New World View, Richard Tarnas, May 2007, Plume, Penguin Group, London, WC2R 0RL, England

7. https://www.metoffice.gov.uk/weather/warnings-and-advice/uk-storm-centre/storm-desmond

8. https://www.bbc.co.uk/news/magazine-19834975

9. https://apps.who.int/iris/bitstream/handle/10665/44102/9789241597906_eng.pdf;jsessionid=76149D636A6FE1922E55A4B9669DF

10. Thich Nhat Hanh Dharma Talks http://www.thhaudio.org[1]

---

1. http://www.thhaudio.org/

Further Reading

The Power of Now: A Guide to Spiritual Enlightenment, Eckhart Tolle, New World Library, August 2004

How to Know Higher Worlds, Rudolph Steiner, 2008, Anthroposophic Press Inc, P.O. Box 749, Gt, Barringotn, MA 01230

The Force, Stuart Wilde, 1997, Hay House Inc, USA

Care of The Soul, How to Add Depth and Meaning to Your Everyday Life, Thomas Moore, 1992, Harper Collins

<u>https://www.maryenglish.com</u>

Also by Mary English

The Astrology of Lovers, How Astrology Can Help You Love Better
The Astrology of Indigos, Everyday Solutions to Spiritual Difficulties
Neptune in Pisces, An Astrological Search for Enlightenment

Watch for more at https://www.maryenglish.com.

Lightning Source UK Ltd.
Milton Keynes UK
UKHW010659160223
417122UK00019B/1741

9 798201 281861